*Writing Handbooks*

# Marketing Your Book: An Author's Guide

*Writing Handbooks*

# Marketing Your Book: An Author's Guide

Alison Baverstock

With a Foreword by Jacqueline Wilson

A & C Black • London

*For Alasdair, Harriet, Jack and Hamish*
*Always my most fruitful source of market research*

First published 2001
A & C Black (Publishers) Limited
37 Soho Square, London W1D 3QZ

© 2001 Alison Baverstock

ISBN 0–7136–5965-3

A CIP catalogue record for this book is available
from the British Library.

Typeset in 10$\frac{1}{2}$ on 12$\frac{1}{2}$ pt Sabon
Printed and bound in Great Britain by
Creative Print and Design (Wales), Ebbw Vale

# Contents

# Foreword
## by Jacqueline Wilson

I certainly wasn't an overnight success as a writer. I had my first children's book published when I was 24. For the next twenty years I wrote around forty books. They all got published – and they mostly sank without trace. How I would have benefited from this brilliant book on marketing in those days!

I got lucky ten years ago. I was invited to write for the publishers of my dreams. They all work as a team and everyone in the firm is very aware of the importance of clever marketing and publicity. If only all publishers could make this kind of effort for all their authors! But this book offers sound practical advice so that authors can do their best themselves to help make their work successful. We'd all like to think that our books are so beguilingly written with such a strong message that they will whiz up those best seller charts by merit alone. Sadly it rarely happens that way. The greatest literary work is not much use if there are just a few copies languishing in a warehouse unread. Even the shyest and most retiring of writers want to communicate. They need an audience. Every book needs to be bought.

Alison Baverstock offers sensible useful tips that will help get our books known and appreciated. Authors often grind their teeth and groan about idle or incompetent publishers. She suggests channelling any irritation into positive action. We have to be grown up and take responsibility for our own manuscripts. We might write 'The End' when we've finished each book – but it's only the *beginning*. Every single author knows the sheer hard work that goes into writing any kind of book. It makes sense to work hard at marketing them too.

This is a treasury of up-to-date inside information, fascinating anecdotes, and imaginative advice. It will only take a couple of hours to read, but the knowledge gained should last a literary lifetime.

# Introduction

Whether you are leafing through this introduction in a bookshop, or have already purchased the book, you may be wondering why it was written in the first place. Why do authors need to know about marketing? Surely that's what publishers are for.

Welcome to the real world. Whilst it's hugely satisfying having a book idea accepted for publication, particularly after years of trying, huge amounts spent on postage, endless rejection letters and the resultant battering of your morale, this is in no way the end of the struggle to gain recognition as an author.

Acceptance of a book by a publishing house is the beginning of a whole new stage, and one during which the author must remain vigilant if their book is to have any chance of success.

It's a common complaint from authors that publishers do not do enough to promote their book. Some even end up wondering why the publisher took the decision to produce the book in the first place if they are so reluctant to help it sell.

At the same time, it won't have escaped your notice that many people commissioned to write books today are not known primarily for their writing ability: their names are well known for something else, and they have turned into (or arguably not) authors with the help of a ghost writer. If writing talent is no longer key to the decision to publish, the role of the author is surely under threat:

> It's not just ageist, but lookist. The younger and more beautiful the author, the more promotable they are as a writer. That has nothing to do with the writing.
>
> Deborah Moggach,
> Chairman of the Society of Authors
> *The Times*, 30 October 2000

The advice contained in this book will be practical, but may be hard hitting at times. I will provide guidelines on how to work with your publisher – and how to get the most out of the relationship. I defend this by saying that I have been on both sides of the fence. I started my working life in publishing, and worked in a variety of marketing, publicity and sales jobs before going freelance ten years ago. Since then I have written several books myself and thus have first-hand experience of how, by working with your publisher, much greater results can be achieved.

From the publisher's side of the fence, it's fair to say that it's not uncommon for authors to overrate their significance as writers. Many know little about the publishing process, how investment decisions are made and what they are up against (for example, how many other titles are being produced in the same period of time as their own). And it is simply not possible within the economics of publishing to provide every book with mass-market advertising.

Authors are often actively disdainful of marketing and commercial forces; indeed many feel that the process of writing thankfully isolates them from the need to get involved. I think this is a big risk to take.

Publishing is a very complex business. A good publisher must be able to estimate public demand, produce the right product before that demand is lost, and then find more of the same to fulfil expectations, whilst relying on the creative (and therefore not necessarily sustainable) powers of third parties to provide the goods. It's a very difficult balancing act.

At the same time, what will or won't work is notoriously difficult to predict. A publishing house may publish six new novels at the same time and have very little chance of knowing which will sell best. Small factors can have a disproportionately large influence on sales. An interview in the right place at the time of publication can be enormously effective, as can a controversial endorsement. Understanding marketing also helps make you more aware of trends outside your world which nevertheless affect your readers and their willingness to buy your books.

I maintain that if you understand the factors that influence public opinion, and lead to sales, you are in a better position to participate in the process and hence be on the receiving end of the beneficial effects. And, of course, if your books are selling well then your share of your publisher's attention is likely to be greater and your long-term future as a writer more secure.

So, having stated the difficulties on both sides, the aim of this book is to explain how marketing works in publishing, and to provide guidance if you decide to work with your publisher. Help is also provided if you decide to manage without the publisher completely and self-publish.

Whether you are a first-time author anxious to make the promotion of your title as effective as possible, or a frequently published author in search of a boost, I hope you will find it useful.

Alison Baverstock

# 1. What Authors Complain About Most

This chapter was not originally meant to be here; it was certainly not part of the synopsis I submitted to my publisher. I had envisaged sprinkling my entire text with references to what authors thought of their publishers, mixing positive and negative comments. But as I began my research, I was overwhelmed by the similarity of authors' reactions.

My research began with an address to a seminar on marketing for members of the Society of Authors. I then approached a number of individuals, asking basic questions about what they thought of publishers and how they felt about how their books were marketed. I was hit by a deluge of negativity, which I felt it my duty to pass on. I do so for two reasons:

(1) some problems were very common, experienced to a greater or lesser degree by almost everyone I spoke to. I outline them in the hope of making those who are reading this understand that they are not alone

(2) to help authors plug the deficiencies in their publishers' marketing systems and thus to improve sales.

## Publishers are useless at communicating with authors. They always know best and won't listen to an author's ideas for marketing their book

- When I approached the marketing department with my ideas for marketing I was invited to go and discuss them in more detail. The head of marketing listened attentively, but once I had left nothing seemed to happen. I felt as though the meeting was designed to humour me and shut me up.

- When I contact the marketing department I get the impression that I am interrupting something far more important and would I please hurry up and go away again.
- Local publicity can be brilliant for selling books – many readers are interested in an author who is local to them. I've found that publishers are completely uninterested in media other than the nationals; they seem to think it's a bit beneath them to deal with regional programmes and papers.
- What's an author publicity form? I've never seen one and this is my fifth book.
- The only way to get on with publishers is to be assertive to the point of aggression.
- I hate what publishers make me like. I have to be pushy. I can feel my ears burning once I have put the phone down. I've had a lifelong resistance to being seen as someone who makes trouble. Apparently rats and humans feel depressed when they have no control over their lives. This is how publishers make authors feel.

## Publishers keep leaving

- It's very difficult to keep track of who does what; staff seem to stay very little time. If it takes 2–3 years to complete a book, I'm likely to have loads of names in my address book by the time the book is finished.
- The editor who had commissioned my book left and I felt both the book and I had been orphaned. No one wanted us any more; we were leftovers. It was very dispiriting.

## Money

- I suppose most authors feel they don't get as much remuneration as they deserve. What really annoys me is the randomness of it all. There is a huge gulf between mega-earning authors and those who scrape by, but the differences between the respective quality of writing being rewarded are never so clear cut.

- Publishers seem to offer what they think they can get away with rather than what they *should* pay. I just wonder how many authors accept the first offer thinking that if they don't they will lose the opportunity to be published at all.
- Being coaxed through the writing process or dealing with editorial queries means you get close to the main contact, usually the editor. But this makes complaining about lack of marketing or publicity, or dealing with the financial side of your next book (if you do not have an agent) very difficult. It's hard to be distant and professional with someone you know well.
- Most authors really want to be published, and that makes it difficult to get fair terms. You get the best negotiated deal when you don't really care about the outcome, but few authors feel that way. The best deal I ever got was when I really didn't care one way or another. I was very busy and asked for what was by my standards an enormous advance. It seems the editor really wanted the book and was prepared to pay.

## Publishers are amateurs

- There is something so gloriously amateurish about publishing. No apparent budgets, and what would seem to be an entirely random process of planning. It often seems to me that money is spent at an illogical time in the book's life-cycle – there is cash around for publication of the hardback which no one can afford, but none left to promote the arrival of the paperback which could use the reviews by now acquired and bring the book to the attention of a much wider audience.
- At one stage I did have a grumble to the editorial team about publicity and sales and they completely agreed with me. Their beef was that they are almost as enthusiastic as the authors about the fiction titles; they spend ages tweaking them, getting the jacket right, writing an appetising blurb, and they too feel somewhat cheated when the books don't sell. Now try imagining an employee in another industry writing this way about their own company *to a client.*

3

- I have recently taken a job in retail, and I notice that in the shop the manager and senior sales assistants are constantly working out strategies to push lines that are selling slowly, to get new stock where it is noticed and to get customers to part with more money than they intended. I am sure that my publisher and her sales team do a lot of this and the authors simply don't see it, but if we were just kept informed now and again of the strategies they have attempted, the chains they have approached only to be rejected . . . I think it is being left in total ignorance of what they are trying to do that makes one feel that nothing is happening, and fear that one's book is being left to rot somewhere.

- Some of my best reviews were missed by the publisher, and I heard of them in a completely random fashion. On one particularly memorable occasion, I heard of a two-page review of my book along with a cover photograph in *The Independent* four months earlier, from a woman I sat next to at my daughter's carol concert.

  I have now found out how to get hold of previously published reviews. You have to ring the paper in question and ask for the Cuttings Library who will give you the date of the review. You then contact Historic Newspapers who will (on payment) send you a copy of the paper. But I really don't see why I should have to know all this in order to see my reviews – I think the publisher should either track what appears, or pay a cuttings agency to do the same. (See Useful Addresses.)

- With my first novel I benefited enormously from my publishing house's decision to venture into producing mass-market paperbacks and I got a relatively large amount of publicity as a result. That coupled with the fact that my first book had a particularly eye-catching cover had given me high (but possibly deluded) hopes of entering the best-seller lists. To then find that most copies of my book seemed to be languishing in a warehouse in Lincolnshire was a bit of a blow. My second book was nominated for the Parker Romantic Novel of the Year. Again there was quite a bit of publicity, but my publisher was so busy trying to revamp the cover of the paperback that it didn't hit the shops until a year after the hardback and six months after the hullabaloo of the award was over.

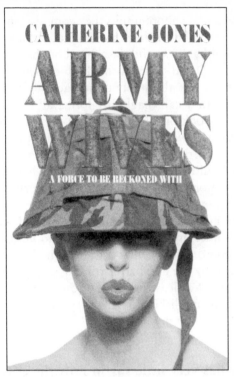

**My first book had a particularly eye-catching cover...**

## Publishers come from too narrow a social circle; consequently they are out of touch with the vast majority of the market

- I come from a lower middle class background. My father was a bank clerk and I went to a state school, although I did go to Oxford. I couldn't believe it when I had my first book published. I entered a world where absolutely everyone had been privately educated and there was no one like me at all. The upper middle classes had corralled a nice working environment, doing something particularly pleasant, entirely to themselves.
- Publishers often seem to be completely out of date. Using words the market no longer recognises; recommending colours and fabrics for cover design that went out ages ago. The

5

look of the author photographs they commission is so dated.

When I describe to them the market I think I write for they look mildly distasteful; fascinated but baffled, as if I am describing a David Attenborough documentary which is interesting but has absolutely no impact on their daily lives – and which they can thankfully forget all about once they have got the book out. None of them ever read *The Sun* or watch *This Morning* and I think that's a pity; they have insufficient experience of the world to sell to it effectively.

- I know it is difficult to sell fiction, but I have found that magazine editors will often buy a short story by someone who has a novel coming out, adding in the details of the book to be published at the end of the piece. I have set this up several times myself. My publisher had no idea this was possible and no media contacts to help me.
- I'm intrigued by the number of reading groups in this country – I know of at least five in the town where I live – and really hope my publisher is trying very hard to reach this key market. I somehow doubt it.

## The author has very little say in how the cover looks

- An author was shown the cover artwork for her book. It showed a blonde girl, who it emerged they thought was the heroine of the story. When the author pointed out that her heroine had black hair, not blonde, she was asked to change the text so this cover artwork could still be used.
- David Cook's historical novel *Sunrising* opens with a pregnant girl knowing that the father of her baby is about to be hanged. During her labour the umbilical cord gets trapped around the child's neck and he suffocates, thus ironically meeting the same fate as his father. The artist commissioned to illustrate the cover had clearly not read (or been briefed by anyone who had read) the entire book, and produced a picture of a girl in a shawl holding a baby. When the author pointed out that this was a nonsense, the publisher's solution was to airbrush out the baby, thus leaving the girl's head in a very funny position and with a very strange expression.

- Margaret Leroy's *Pleasure* is a serious examination of female sexuality. The publisher insisted on putting an erotic picture of a thin, naked woman on the front cover. The author protested that not only was this inappropriate, but it was also ridiculous given the book's content. One of the key points she makes is that an ampler figure allows a heightened sexual experience. She was ignored, and her request for a male nude on the cover was rejected outright. But the inappropriate jacket was widely commented on both by reviewers (largely female) and purchasers (again largely female: 'I felt so embarrassed reading your book in public because of the cover image').

## Publishers' literary ambitions

- Publishers often seem to have ambitions to be authors themselves. That's what makes them such a poor judge of other people's talent. Because they are so often thinking 'that's not the way I'd write it', their instincts get in the way of spotting stories that *other* people want to read.

## Publishers have no understanding of how it feels to be the author

- Publishers have no understanding at all of just how much effort goes into writing a book.

  I worked for six months on preparing a revised edition of my book. Although I got a small advance for the new book, my editor insisted we call it a 'revised edition' rather than a 'new edition' because there was less than one-third new material, and that apparently was the 'industry standard'. After sending off my extensive revisions, I heard nothing, and then was surprised to be asked to sign a copy of the new edition on a course I was teaching. I contacted the publisher to find out if one had yet been sent to me and was told that I did not qualify – I was only entitled to a free copy of a 'new edition', not a 'revised edition'. I was stunned. Apart from thinking them exceptionally mean, it seemed to demonstrate such a fundamental misunderstanding about whose work it was.

# 2. What is Marketing?

I'm a firm believer in definitions. If you define precisely what you are talking about then you have more chance of both setting realistic objectives and achieving your aims.

Nowhere is this more important than in marketing. Marketing often presents an image of chaotic flurry: too much money being spent in apparently random pursuit of the unattainable. But true marketing is the calculated application of resources where they are most likely to yield effect.

So, we will start with an understanding of marketing theory and then proceed with a description of how this relates to the promotion of books.

Definitions of marketing are particularly problematic. Academics cannot agree and many articles have been written discussing what marketing means. I also think that because marketing is a relatively new discipline for academic study, it has been overafflicted by verbiage: the desire of those working in the subject to provide an appropriate (and some would say impenetrable) vocabulary to elevate the subject. It seems to me that relatively new academic disciplines such as sociology, art history and marketing are much more prone to this than more established subjects such as history and English.

Equally unhelpful are the demotic – but far more memorable – terms associated with marketing via the media: 'hoodwinked', 'conned', 'suckered', 'landed with', as well as the range of consumer interest programmes with the basic message that anyone selling anything is most likely trying to con you.

It is certainly true that many authors feel a genuine distaste for the commercial, and an even greater disdain for the associated language. Even if you too have little liking for marketing and marketing speak, try to remember the following two points:

(1) Most people enjoy spending money
It's quite common to see purchasing described as 'retail therapy'.
As journalist Ruth Picardie wrote, when dying of cancer:

> Essentially, after months of careful research, I have discovered a treatment that is a) cheaper than complementary therapy b) a hell of a lot more fun than chemotherapy and c) most important, incredibly effective! Retail therapy! . . . Thanks to this highly evolved, only moderately expensive and largely side-effect free treatment, I am currently in almost no pain! . . . My non-beard book, *Shop Yourself out of Cancer*, is coming soon.[1]

(2) Books are very reasonably priced
For the would-be book-buyer the financial entry point is low and the purchase could be the start of a long-term relationship. Even those who buy a book that they subsequently find they hate emerge with that most useful of social assets: an opinion.

## A very basic definition of marketing

Marketing means effective selling: making your sales proposal to the market so appealing that a decision to purchase results.

Obviously the definition will vary according to whether it is a product, service or information that you are making available, and the response you want from the market (purchase, decision, recommendation, donation, and so on). But this basic definition will serve us very well.

For the author, it is helpful to think of marketing in terms of making the potential market for a book aware of the product and then encouraging them to purchase.

Now let's break down this definition further and pull out various threads of argument. There are several useful checklists for doing so – you may well be familiar with the formula of Ps: people, product, promotion, place, price, personnel, and so on. I would like to offer the following subheadings; the first four

---

[1] *Before I Say Goodbye*, Ruth Picardie, Penguin, 1998

are courtesy of Professor Baker of Strathclyde University, the last two are my own.

### Marketing means focusing on the customer

This is the one thing everyone does agree on. Every marketing definition I have ever seen mentions the word 'customer'.

So, thinking about this from the author's point of view, what kind of people buy your books and why? Don't assume that they are all like you. I heard Margaret Atwood recently describe her readers as hugely diverse, defying any group categorisation, and that this had been realised through her very large and varied postbag. She summed them up as 'Dear Reader'.

If your titles are aimed at a specific market (for example, educational or professional) then categorising your readers becomes much easier, but there are still a range of questions that you should be asking yourself. (And it's you that should be doing the asking rather than the publisher because your overall market knowledge will be better than theirs.)

- At what stage in their professional career will they benefit from your book?
- How will they use it? What needs (current or future) will it meet?
- What job title do they have? This will probably need several variants – try to provide them all.
- What professional associations do they belong to and how often do they meet up? Can you obtain the relevant lists of members?

### Marketing needs a long perspective

Effective marketing cannot be achieved overnight. It takes detailed thought, and thought takes time.

If your publisher were to double the amount spent on your marketing tomorrow, you would probably not see the effect on sales by next week. It might even produce the opposite effect, as spending too much money on a promotion can alienate a market. For example, imagine making a decision to increase the production specification (in other words, improve the overall quality of the materials being used) for a mailshot appealing for money for starving children. The most likely result would be to alienate the market; it would look as if too much had been spent on production, and therefore less had reached the children in need.

Along the same lines, think about how long a promotion piece is going to be around for and whether contemporary events referred to in the leaflet will date or change in how they are perceived. For example, I do some work for the publisher of a range of CDs of church music. In April 2000 I deleted the reference to one particular choir boy having 'sung at the Dome on Millennium Night'. By then the press was in full negative chorus about the Dome and it was no longer a selling point.

In addition, watch out for words that, although currently popular, are likely to date. If your material must last a long time, the words must too.

## Effective marketing means using all the resources at your disposal

Effective marketing means using all the resources of a company to promote sales, not just those of one department. In practice, this means that the various departments within a publishing house should be communicating and working towards the same end.

Certain publishing houses are known to produce particular kinds of books. Thus, simply saying that a poetry title comes from Bloodaxe, or a music-teaching title from A&C Black, means that it will get greater respect from the market and those reviewing it than would be the case if they had never heard of the publisher.

If you become aware of animosity between different departments or contacts at your particular publishing house[2], you will have to work doubly hard to ensure the information you send in is seen by all who need access to it – it's probably best to send two copies!

## Marketing means being both innovative and flexible

This is true of marketing in all fields. We tire quickly and are eager for the new and different. Some of the recent marketing successes flew in the face of conventional wisdom, for example

[2]See Chapter 1, page 3

initial market research on the Sony Walkman was not positive, as the benefits of a tape recorder into which you could not record were not seen.

Some of publishing's big successes in recent years have been, on first examination, very unlikely – think of *Longitude*. When there are so many different titles competing for attention in bookshops, what can really make a new one stand out? In the case of *Longitude*, however interesting the story, it was surely the book's attractive format and sheer possessability, as well as the attractive price, that helped start the sales phenomenon.

It is also important to keep track of what else consumers spend their money on, and how these products are marketed. So start reading your 'junk mail', ask people you meet what they think of bookshops and read advertisements for products in the street. I find my children an endlessly fertile source of market research.

### Marketing depends on relationships

This seems to me a point of fundamental importance. Effective marketing builds up relationships between all those you wish to include: shareholders, purchasers, existing and potential employees.

This point seems to me to apply with particular force in publishing. The relationship between reader and writer lasts a long time, as the book is read, and then remembered. And the deeper the experience inspired by the book (whether positive or negative) the truer this is.

Writers report that the letters they receive from readers can be incredibly perceptive, and websites also attest to the involvement felt – some raising copyright issues when ideas develop so far from the original creator.

The same goes for relationships with publishing houses. For example, I remember when the Virago books first appeared. I loved the books themselves (Rosamund Lehmann and Radclyffe Hall were two authors I discovered this way) and also the format – the rich green, largish print and beautiful cover images. Virago published authors who were out of print and forgotten, and I bought many. They then seemed to start publishing books which, although still beautifully packaged, were perhaps deservedly out of print. I lost confidence and, after a couple of unenjoyable reads, never bought a Virago paperback again. This was not a vindictive decision, and not something I realised until years later. It was just that my confidence was dented and I started to look elsewhere – so other authors undoubtedly benefited from my change of allegiance.

Lastly, remember that relationships do not have to be good to be remembered. Memories in the book business can be very long, as those who have negatively reviewed books will be aware.

### Marketing is logical
This means thinking about what you are trying to achieve and then attempting to achieve your goals, and is best done by planning.

As you become involved with a publishing house you enter a world of new words and formats. My hope is that this book will help; the Glossary lists and explains commonly heard terms. You may be confused about the range of promotional materials that publishing houses produce, but in Chapter 4 I describe each and the logic behind it, so that if asked to contribute to or comment on the copy, you understand why it is being created.

## Particular problems that those selling books have to confront

### Competition
As authors we are committed to thinking books are wonderful. Whilst there are many who agree with us, sadly there are even more who find the book irrelevant, as the following quotation reveals:

> I don't really read books: there's not enough space in my life. When I have an empty space in my brain, it's cool, it's OK. I don't want to fill it with anything.
> Celine Dion, singer,
> *Sunday Times Magazine*, October 1999

Books have to compete with a vast range of other items that cost about the same – or perhaps more – but take less decision-making time. Nor is one book always competing with another title for the customer's money. An alternative to buying a book could be a training course (costing vastly more) or a meal out; the customer is not necessarily deciding between two books.

### Books are worthy, boring necessities

Generations of schoolchildren have grown up with a view of books as boring necessities associated with homework. The dilapidated condition of the book stock in schools, and poor access (class sets often consist of one between two rather than one each) has compounded this problem.

There are definite ways in which the author can help here. Subheadings encourage the reader to get involved, as do page layouts that reflect modern design, for example with boxes, quotes highlighted and 'sound-bites'. A study of magazine layout will yield further examples.

### Book purchase takes ages

Choosing a book demands a great investment of time – and this is true whether one is a book buyer in a bookshop, or a consumer trying to choose between the titles they have selected. And the time one has to invest – to read the blurb, look at the cover, perhaps read the first paragraph, look at the index, and so on – is in inverse proportion to the financial investment required, for most books sell for a relatively low purchase price.

> Choosing a new item of clothing can take me seconds: do I like the colour, is my size available, is it machine washable? Ironically, the final purchase price can be ten times that of a paperback book that it takes me ten times longer to choose.
>
> Waterstones customer

> I realised that the amount of time I invested in each customer: getting to know them; building a relationship; recommending titles they might like and ordering what I did not have in stock was probably yielding about 20p per title sold. As I was running my bookshop as a business and not, as many of my customers assumed, as a hobby,

14

this was hardly a cost effective way of making a living.
                    Recently retired independent bookseller

How can the author help guide the reader to what they want
to know quickly? By providing concise and interesting information on both the book and yourself whenever possible!

> It never ceases to amaze me the amount of useless person-
> al information an individual will give a reporter – about
> the committees they serve on, whether they are chairman,
> treasurer or secretary, how many clubs they belong to.
> The very grandest will airily hand you a photocopy of
> their entry in *Who's Who*. It is far better that you, rather
> than the reporter, should decide what you think is rele-
> vant. From your obviously glittering and lengthy CV
> choose the few – very few or better still no more than two
> – facts that seem to be most germane to the interview in
> hand. The object of the exercise is to make sure that you
> are seen as the right person to be talking about this issue.

> (drafted as advice for talking to reporters, but equal-
> ly relevant to any form of author information!)
>                                              Peter Hobday,
>                      *Managing the Message*, Allison and Busby

### Customers only buy the same book once

If you decide you like a particular brand of chocolate, or spirit, you will go on buying the same brand until you change your
mind, which may be never. Publishers seldom have the same
opportunity. There are occasions when a title is bought again,
for example as a present, but these are relatively rare. Each
book is a different product, hence the desire of publishing
houses to build a brand to represent a particular type of author
or house. That is why your book may end up looking relatively similar to others the house produces.

### The publisher can never be sure when books are sold

Given the number of titles available, and the importance of
persuading booksellers to stock books by authors who are

completely unknown, the practice developed of supplying books to shops on 'sale or return'. In other words, if books do not sell, they may be returned by the bookseller to the publisher for a credit. But the publisher cannot return them to the printer.

Thus, unlike any other form of retailing, the risk remains with the producer rather than the shop owner. This makes the finances of running a publishing company particularly difficult – you can never tell when the product is actually sold. The nightmare scenario for publishers is that the books have been subscribed into bookshops, the reviews are good, and you order a reprint just as the stock comes back from the shops for a credit.

### Books are outstandingly good value for money

In industry, most firms would seek to make a profit of at least 15–20 per cent; publishing houses do well to get 5–10 per cent. As some wag once said, the only enterprise you take on for love not money is owning either a publishing house or a football team.

I think it behoves all authors to constantly restate the value that book purchase represents. A paperback novel costs less than a takeaway meal or a large frozen chicken, yet there are still large sections of society that consider them expensive.

So, can you deliberately buy books (rather than anything else) as presents, give a talk in your local library or school to coincide with National Book Week, choose books to be photographed with, or just enthuse about them whenever possible? As we are producers of the codex, our aim should surely be to convert others to feel as John Simpson does when asked what single medium he could not live without:

> Books. Nothing – not radio, nor television, and not even the Internet – can replace the book for me. If books stop being published, I shall give up travelling, close the door and spend the rest of my life reading the ones that already exist. And I shan't switch on the television set, ever again.
> John Simpson, BBC Chief Foreign Correspondent,
> *The Times*, 3 November 2000

# 3. How to Get Your Manuscript Noticed by a Publishing House

An early stage of marketing your book is getting it accepted for publication by a publishing house. This is where authors really need determination – lots of people finish books, but the number of those who determinedly keep going until they find a publisher is far fewer.

Look through a writers' directory such as the *Writers' and Artists' Yearbook* (A&C Black) and you may find the number of houses that exist daunting. Which should you approach?

## What kind of book is it?

Visit a bookshop and decide in what section your book might sit, and in what company. Then look to see who publishes in this area. Note down the names of the firms involved in order to contact them.

## Which authors write the kind of book you have in mind?

Thinking about who else writes your kind of book is a very useful way of categorising your writing. As so many new titles come out each year (over 100,000 in the UK alone), publishers often try to sell a new name on the back of an established one, so new writers may find the line 'In the tradition of Catherine Cookson' or 'The new John Grisham' on the front cover of their book. Such comparisons do not have to be book-related, and may have more street cred if they are not, as the following description of a new children's book from Puffin shows:

'*Die Hard* with Fairies'[1].

Do the thinking on this for your potential publisher. Without being ridiculous (avoid comparisons with Shakespeare, and don't make an easy-to-read thriller sound like Salman Rushdie), with whom could your writing logically be compared?

## Get some feedback on your work

If you are writing for children, ask a parent to read your stories aloud and give you a pithy comment. Or ask children to provide you with a quotation on why they liked it. Do you know any famous people who could provide an introduction or an endorsement that would be significant to the marketability of your book? If you have had your novel read by friends, ask them what they thought of it.

## The right kind of publishing house

Most publishing houses specialise. There are very few that publish poetry, and not all publish fiction. Being specialist allows them to penetrate the market more successfully – they will have built up good links with reviewers and the book trade in their area of specialisation and the latter will consequently take seriously titles under their imprint. So offering them a title when they publish no others in that area would be a hard act to pull off, because they have no in-house expertise in that field. (Don't assume that you are helpfully extending their range for them; they may not want it extended!)

Directories of publishing houses list their specialisations, and how they like material to be submitted. Many will not accept unsolicited manuscripts, while some insist on you sending return postage. Remember that the manuscript is sent at your own risk – never send your only copy.

[1]*Artemis Fowl* by Eoin Colfer, Puffin, 2001

## The 'slush pile'

Most publishing houses receive a huge number of unsolicited manuscripts every day. Collectively they are often known as the 'slush pile'. There are stories of manuscripts being taken from the slush pile and turned into best-sellers, but it has to be said that these are told because they are so unusual. The more you can do to help yourself get to the top of the pile the better.

### *How to attract the attention of those reading the slush pile*

Most publishing houses pay readers to go through these manuscripts and deliver a judgement on whether or not they are saleable. Thus your manuscript may never be read by a member of staff from the house you wish to consider you.

The judgement of the readers is not infallible (the *Harry Potter* series was rejected by many of them) and is also under siege because they tend to read so many bad submissions. It follows that those authors who, as well as asking to be published, also indicate who might buy their books, are at an immediate advantage.

So, on a single side of A4 paper that accompanies your publishing idea, outline its marketing potential. Try to answer the following questions:

- what is it? Romantic novel or business manual, travel guide or 'how to' self-help book?
- what are your qualifications to write it? Try to keep these brief, relevant and interesting, using emotive language (for example, 'author detests dogs' rather than 'author is afraid of dogs')
- what will this book do better than any other source of information/enjoyment available? Can you quantify these benefits? For example, 'buying a copy of this manual will save the purchaser thousands of pounds in accountancy fees'
- what kind of people will buy it? Can you define them clearly (job title, social standing, what they watch or read, etc.)?
- how much disposable income (or budget if it's a professional title) do they have?
- how many are there of them and how contactable are they?

The latter is crucial – a targetable society or mailing list is the genesis of many a published product. It doesn't matter if the resulting market is small in size, just that their desire or need for the product, and ability to purchase, are real
- what trends in society does your book highlight – for example, news events, popular concerns, audience viewing figures/magazine circulation of relevant publications? Has anyone notable said anything in support of this recently? If there's been a pithy article in the press about the same subject, attach a photocopy as proof, with the key sections underlined or highlighted.

### How marketable are you as an author?
Your own marketability as an author is also very important to the decision-making process. A publisher may be unduly swayed by whether they think you will obtain publicity at the time of publication, so if you sound interesting here it can be a great help.

Trawl through your CV, thinking about what you have done in the past that is relevant – this could be something you have written, taken part in or even decried. For example:

- any time spent in a retail environment will have taught you that people can be very fickle
- have you had letters published somewhere relevant?
- have you had to research or write reports (perhaps as part of your job) for a wide circulation? This shows you can get to the bottom of a tricky situation and explain it clearly
- time in a playgroup or being a mother will have taught you how to manage your time, in what little regard the rest of the population hold you, and that trying to keep the attention of small children is difficult
- any experience of PR (for a new playground, to stop a road) will have revealed how important it is to identify and then get through to certain taste barons who have huge influence
- have you given any interviews on local radio? This is very good practice for promoting a book.

Professional CV writers specialise in turning quite ordinary work or life experiences into significant-sounding events, so try to do the same.

## The Society of Authors

Once you have a book accepted for publication you are eligible to join the Society of Authors, and this is a very wise move. As well as regular meetings they also offer a contract checking service – a detailed examination of the legal terms of publication which is immensely useful. An agent can do this too, but the Society's advice is free (see Useful Addresses).

## Using an agent

All well-known authors seem to have agents, and finding an agent to take you on and present your book idea to possible publishers is a huge advantage.

### How to find an agent

Look through a book trade yearbook and you will find lists of agents as well as the kinds of books in which they specialise. Many agents are former publishers, and so the tips for presenting material apply equally to them. Bear in mind too that:

- they do not need to see a complete manuscript before considering your book proposal. They can make a decision on your literary style and likely marketability by reading a few sample chapters (for fiction) or studying the contents list and your personal information
- whilst most agents do not charge a reading fee, you will pay them a percentage of both your advance (lump sum paid to authors at the beginning of a contract, based on likely eventual sales or desirability of the author in question) and your eventual sales. Most charge you a percentage of the royalties (often 10 per cent for home sales and 20 per cent for overseas) but you should check the terms in the contract offered.

21

# 4. How Marketing Works in Publishing

Marketing is much more important to publishers today than used to be the case. Until about ten years ago, the industry was editorially dominated; most of the early decisions about the manuscript were taken on the basis of content, with discussion of how to make the product sell starting much later.

Today, the vast majority of publishing houses in Britain are led by people from a marketing background. With books being sold through a much greater variety of locations (for example, supermarkets, garage forecourts, leisure centres and restaurants), the marketing of books has *had* to become more professional. This is having a substantial impact on the kind of titles commissioned. Rather than being a product-driven industry – where products are created before the search for markets begins – the industry is now increasingly market-driven. Publishers try to identify market segments with specific needs, and then to produce the products to match.

## Marketing in publishing: what and when?

Most publishing houses divide responsibility for different parts of the publishing process between different departments (*editorial* for content, *marketing* for sales, *production* for format, *distribution* for the mechanics of getting the books where they are needed). It is usual for senior staff from each of these departments (or perhaps just the appropriate director) to get together at regular intervals to discuss and then hopefully approve the plan to publish new titles. It is at these meetings that the idea for a new title will be approved, and to which a plan for its marketing and the overall size of the market will be introduced.

For each title that comes up, the marketing director will be required to say how many they estimate are likely to be sold. It is in this way that the title's print run is established.

Once a forthcoming title has been approved by this meeting, and money can be spent on it, the title's marketing will be broken down into a series of stages that will be carried out by more junior members of the department. In general, most of the following are routine procedures (those only relevant to books for which there are particularly high expectations are described as such).

### House database

All titles need basic descriptive copy for a range of purposes, from catalogue compilation to in-house newsletters, long before the accompanying manuscript has been delivered. It will be loaded onto the house computer system (or database) and recycled many times.

This first piece of descriptive copy about your book will probably be drafted by your sponsoring editor, based on the information you submitted to the house in a bid to be published. It should state both your title's and your own key selling points.

This is not the place for a complete biography; rather just two or three key attributes that qualify you to write the title in question are needed.

The most important thing is to ensure that this copy remains up-to-date. Database copy is drafted very early in a book's life, and the content of the final book may change dramatically during the writing process. By final delivery, the title, publication date and even author name may have changed.

### Author's publicity form

This will be sent to the author and should be filled in by you (see Chapter 5). This is usually sent out about the same time as your contract, but may be forgotten about, so be sure to ask for one.

### An advance notice (or advance information sheet/forthcoming title sheet. The title varies from house to house).

An advance notice is routinely produced for each new book and will be sent to all who need to know about it (bookshops, reps and wholesalers, overseas offices, and so on). This is the first public information on the forthcoming title and usually appears 6–9 months pre-publication. The usual format is an A4 sheet, with the subject matter broken down under a series of headings (author, title, short piece of information on the title, publication details such as format and price).

# ADVANCE

## INFORMATION

A&C BLACK

Australia

## Australia

A major new Blue Guide to one of the world's 'hottest' destinations. The Blue Guide is the first ever historical and cultural guide to Australia.

Indispensable to travellers, the Blue Guide is also a mine of information for those simply fascinated by this amazing country.

Australia offers a unique combination of natural wonders, expansive wilderness and cosmopolitan cities. Blue Guide Australia provides visitors with an unprecendented introduction to this culture. There are introductory articles on Australian art, literature and film, as well as natural history, Aboriginal culture and history.

The main text, organised by state, includes extensive practical information for the tourist. The walking tours of the towns and cities are interspersed with stories of historical figures, cultural events and literary sites.

**KEY SELLING POINTS**

• the first guidebook to focus on Australia's rich culture

• compiled by experts

• walking tours of towns and cities

• put together in a readable style

• detailed maps and plans

• extensive practical information

| SUBJECT | EDITION | BINDING | FORMAT (mm) | EXTENT | ILLUSTRATIONS |
|---------|---------|---------|-------------|--------|---------------|
| Travel | 1st | paperback | 195x123 | 608pp | 35 illustrations colour map 40 maps & plans |

## Author(s)

**Erika Esau and George Boeck are originally from the USA but have settled in Australia. They describe writing the Blue Guide as a love letter to their new country. They live in Canberra. Erika is a Lecturer in Art History at the Australian National University, while George works in the Research section of the Australian Institute of Aboriginaland TorresStrait Islander Studies.**

PRICE £15.99

ISBN 0 7136 3846 X

PUBLICATION DATE AUGUST 1999

| AUTHOR LOCATION | US PUBLISHER | CANADA? |
|-----------------|--------------|---------|
| CANBERRA, AUSTRALIA | NORTON | PENGUIN CANADA |

ISBN 0-7136-3846-X

9 780713 638462

A & C Black (Publishers) Limited, PO Box 19, Huntingdon, Cambs PE19 8SF tel: 01480 212666 fax: 01480 405014 email:sales@acblackdist.com
Editorial, publicity and rights: 37 Soho Square, London W1D 3QZ tel: 020 7758 0200 fax: 020 7758 0222 email:enquiries@acblack.com

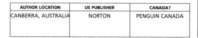

**A sample advance information sheet**

## GALAPAGOS DIARY

This is quite simply a breathtaking book – or rather two books in one!

World famous bird illustrator Hermann Heinzel teamed up with a young photographer to capture the bird and other wildlife of these extraordinary islands. The first section of the book is a tour around each of the islands describing in words, illustrations and photographs the habitats and wildlife to be found, highlighting some of the strange breeding strategies of the archipelago's birds with breathtaking – and often amusing – illustrations.

The second half of the book is a detailed 'field guide' with sketches and more finished paintings, photographs and maps – a fresh approach to the conventional field guide which makes the pages alive and 'buzzing'.

**KEY SELLING POINTS**

• Two books in one! A tour of the islands and field guide

• 640+ colour photos, thousands of colour illustrations

• Illustrated by one of Europe's most famous bird artists

| SUBJECT | EDITION | BINDING | FORMAT (mm) | EXTENT | ILLUSTRATIONS |
|---|---|---|---|---|---|
| ORNITHOLOGY | FIRST | PAPER | 239 X 167 | 272 | thousands of colour dwgs, colour maps, 640 col photos |

### Author(s)

**Hermann Heinzel** has been involved with birds and bird illustration for more years than he cares to remember. He is the illustrator of one of the most successful European field guides ever published – *Birds of Britain and Europe* (HarperCollins). He has travelled widely and worked for TV, magazines and book publishers on many varied and exciting projects.

**Barnaby Hall** is now a student at Duke University in the USA. This is his first book.

| PRICE |
|---|
| £14.99 |

| ISBN |
|---|
| 0-7136-5434-1 |

| PUBLICATION DATE |
|---|
| SEPTEMBER 2000 |

| AUTHOR LOCATION | US PUBLISHER | CANADA? |
|---|---|---|
| HEINZEL = FRANCE HALL = USA | UNIV CALIFORNIA PRESS | NO |

A & C Black (Publishers) Limited, PO Box 19, Huntingdon, Cambs PE19 3SF tel: 01480 212666 fax: 01480 405014 email:sales@acblackdist.co.uk
Editorial, publicity and rights: 35 Bedford Row, London WC1R 4JH  tel: 0171 242 0946  fax: 0171 831 8478  email:enquiries@acblack.co.uk

The basic difference from the house database information is the inclusion of a sales prediction. This document should include any information that gives an idea of how many copies are likely to be sold, and will thus encourage the retailer to stock the book. This could include:

- sales of author's last title
- key trends in the media/society that highlight the subject matter with relevant audience/population figures
- publicity/promotion already arranged to support demand
- details of location of story or author which may help persuade local stockists to take more.

### Catalogue entry

Almost all publishing houses produce catalogues at regular intervals: an annual catalogue with a listing of all the new titles; a complete catalogue listing everything in print (often does not include blurbs); seasonal lists in-between (usually spring/summer and autumn/winter) that give details of the highlights of that particular period.

These act as a shop window for the wares of a particular publisher. Entries in these publications may be short – perhaps just a paragraph or two – but they will still routinely reach the 3,300 bookshops and key wholesalers in Britain, and the many outlets stocking English language titles overseas. What's more important, they are kept and referred to long after receipt – especially by customer order departments and by shops who never get a visit from a representative.

Catalogues are used for year-round reference so the copy needs to last and not be dependent on time-specific information. They also present the company's wares alongside each other, so it is important that the words used to describe each title:

- make its specific benefits clear
- do not knock other titles (either directly or by implication, for example saying that a particular diet book is the only one the reader will ever need, if the company publishes ten others)
- build the publishing house's reputation for a particular type of book. The author can ride on the back of this; they may gain new readers out of the staple band who know a particular imprint and trust it.

### Presentation at sales conferences

Many publishing houses use sales representatives to call (either physically or by phone) on retail outlets stocking books. Most houses brief their reps twice or three times a year, providing them with binders that list the forthcoming titles over that period, and any key facts that may help them to persuade retailers to stock.

Very occasionally the author may be asked to talk to the reps – this is a valuable opportunity. If you are asked to talk to the reps, a 'performance' will be more memorable than a long description of what is in the book. Wear something bright and try to provide a couple of anecdotes that they can use when calling on shops.

### Presenters

Presenters are glossy, very high quality brochures that are used to draw a response from booksellers, wholesalers and key accounts (for example, Waterstones and Books Etc). They are not produced for every title, just those for which publishers have high expectations.

With very little time in which to impress a book's saleability on a buyer, an effective presenter can draw the appropriate 'wow' and the consequent stock order.

Presenter copy is likely to be very short on book content and author information, and will include greater detail on how the title will be promoted and proof that this will work (based on the success of previous/similar titles).

### Key account presentations

The purchasing power of the major retailers (WH Smiths, Waterstones, and some supermarket chains) and the book wholesalers (notably Gardners, Bertrams and THE) is enormous today, and special visits are arranged to brief them on the titles most likely to appeal. These are usually handled by the Sales (or Key Accounts) Manager, who takes along a marketing outline, cover artwork and author information and a copy of the presenter. Such is their buying power that it is not unusual for a cover design to be altered if an alternative version would produce a larger stock order.

### Leaflets and flyers (simple leaflets)

Leaflets and flyers produced for books are usually as multi-purpose as possible. The publisher will probably not be able to afford to produce a separate flyer for each occasion on which one is needed, but will try to produce stock which will meet most needs. For example, the same leaflet could be handed out at exhibitions, used as the basis of a mailshot (probably with the addition of an accompanying letter and a reply envelope), sent to interested enquirers, and given to authors for their own use. If you really want leaflets that detail a special offer for a particular occasion, it might be cheaper to sticker existing stock than produce a special reprint.

### Direct marketing

Direct marketing means sending a sales message direct to the person most likely to make the buying decision, and cutting out the retailer in the middle. It's a very effective way to sell specialist titles, but works less well for general interest books because of the difficulties of pinpointing and then contacting exactly who you are trying to talk to.

Effective direct marketing copy is divided into smallish paragraphs, uses a simple vocabulary and is quite repetitive, because the market will seldom read anything from start to finish, preferring to 'dot around'. There is a real art to writing an effective direct mail piece, so before you protest that what you have been sent to look at does not reflect your book, do compare it with other direct mail shots.

Direct marketing also includes telemarketing, 'off-the-page' advertising (advertising space with a coupon for the reader to respond), websites and house to house calling.

### Trade advertising

Advertising in the trade press forms a major part of most publishers' marketing. Space may be taken in the *Bookseller* or *Publishing News*, to reach booksellers and persuade them to stock. In addition, twice a year the publishers of the *Bookseller* magazine (Whitakers) publish export or 'buyer' editions – huge additional volumes that list all the titles in the forthcoming season. As well as submitting editorial copy and author/cover photographs for their future titles, many publishers take up the option of advertising their books as well.

The logic behind an effective trade advertisement is to persuade the retailer to stock, so the copy will concentrate on anticipated demand for the title and the author's ability to deliver what the market wants, rather than specific details of the title in question.

In addition to advertising to reach the trade, publishers may put loose inserts in trade magazines or mail them directly, perhaps concentrating on those shops which specialise in the kind of book they are promoting. The Booksellers Association can supply labels for such a mailing (see Useful Addresses).

## Press advertising

Theory: advertisements in the press reach readers and persuade them to buy. Fact: there are now so many new media formats (for example, the vast range of magazines and broadcast programmes) that planning a 'media schedule' (or list of where and when to advertise) to reach the entire market is both virtually impossible and hugely expensive. More press advertising is the one promotional item that most authors say they want. But many houses are now devoting attention to securing features through promotional arrangements (reader offers and sponsored editorial in return for advertising).

Space advertising (or taking poster sites) can work very well on transport sites – in the carriages of underground trains, on the sides of buses and poster sites in the street.

## Promotions

'Promotions' is a loose term usually referring to the linking of two or more items for a joint push to a related market. For example, newspaper readers might be asked to collect tokens from consecutive issues of a paper towards a free book, or a promotion might be run offering subsidised books on the back of a cereal packet, in return for collecting packet tops. As books have a high perceived value and are seldom thrown away, they offer strong potential for use in promotions.

### Publicity and PR

Book review columns offer a straightforward way to get coverage for a new book. But many forms of media will be more interested in the author than the book, and feature space may be available for author publicity.

On writing a book a wide range of panellist/interviewee opportunities opens up: those who have written about a subject are assumed to be experts. Be aware that little details you would rather were forgotten, or which undermine your seriousness as an expert, may be hugely useful to those handling publicity. For example, what you have on your mantlepiece, the details of your first sexual experience, and how you feel about your childhood all form the basis for regular features in the press in which authors may appear.

For further information see Chapter 8.

### Websites

Most publishing houses now have a website for which they may ask authors to submit relevant information. If you have the chance to provide details about you and your book:

- begin by looking at their website as a whole; your contribution should mirror what is there to be sympathetic to the reader
- don't provide too much – reading on screen is tiring
- do provide interesting information, details that offer added value to what they already have access to. Most readers can spot a book blurb or jacket copy and if they are searching the website for more information, regurgitating what they have already seen is dull.

### Point of sale

This is the term (often abbreviated to POS) that refers to the large-scale reminders to purchase that appear where high profile books are to be sold. Items include multiple copy holders (dump bins), showcards, posters, balloons, and so on.

Because they must be legible throughout the store, the number of words that appear on them will be few. The prominent panel at the top of a dump bin may not include the author's name or book title. This is sensible, as your book will appear many times face front beneath.

## Merchandising
In a publishing context, this means selling further goods to the public which build on the success of the original book. For example, stationery, T-shirts, lunchboxes, soft toys, all of which refer to the original product. Some bookshops have the space to stock these items, but they particularly appeal to other retail outlets such as superstores and serve to expand the 'shelf space' devoted to your book.

## Other marketing activities
There are other routine marketing activities. For example, publishers attend international book fairs, and the British Council takes relevant titles to exhibitions abroad. Many publishers advertise in the marketing materials put out by wholesalers and retailers, and others will take advertising space in relevant publications (for example, *The Times Literary Supplement* or *The Times Educational Supplement*), listing all the titles they are publishing over a specific period.

# 5. What the Author Can Do to Help Promote a Book

Good communication between author and publishing house is the best way of producing effective marketing for the forthcoming book. Whoever is going to publish your book, the best results will be achieved by working together.

So, whether your path to the publishing house has been relatively straightforward, littered with disappointments from this and other houses, or if you have been turned down by hundreds of publishing houses and are absurdly grateful to now be offered a contract by this one, put the past behind you. The best results will be achieved by working methodically with this publisher, not refighting old battles.

Given that:

- no other industry produces as many new products a year, or offers its employees so little time (or money) with which to market them, and
- all books receive basic attention (catalogue entry and advance notice, information on the database),

your aim is to ensure that you get the maximum possible in-house attention and consequently the best possible resulting sales.

## Why do you want to be published?

Spend a few minutes thinking about this rather obvious question. It will help you establish priorities. For example, do you want this book to be published:

- because you have a burning desire to write and your career as a writer depends on being published
- to support other activities such as lecturing or training or your general professional development; a book gives credibility to your wider profile.

According to the rationale provided above, you may be looking for a variety of different kinds of support from your publisher.

---

As a new fiction author you might want the publishers to help with:

- listing in their promotional materials and linking you with appropriate other (and better known) authors, for example 'the new Joanna Trollope'
- finding a suitable endorsement for your title from someone well-known, which will encourage the possibly interested to pick up your book
- leaflets to hand out if you undertake speaking engagements
- a cover blurb and cover that really appeal to the market
- inclusion in relevant trade promotions, for example Christmas catalogues
- enthusiastic presentation to the reps with anecdotes to ensure they remember your title and pass on the right information to get it stocked in shops.

If your book supports a training course you might want the publishers to help with:

- flyers to hand out when training
- an attractive bulk purchase deal to allow you to sell your title as part of training packages
- very efficient delivery of the same so you can rely on them to get the books where and when they are needed
- relevant advertising in professional magazines
- inclusion in direct marketing promotions aimed at the right market
- liaison with book retailers active in this market
- a cover and blurb that reinforce the image you are trying to create and appeal to the market.

---

## The author's publicity form

This is your main chance to impress on the publisher the various reasons why *they* agreed to publish *your* book. You will be asked for information on what you have done and how that relates to the title planned, to provide a short 'blurb' (written description for promotional purposes) about yourself and the book, and for other relevant information. The form should be sent to you at around the same time as your contract, so if you don't get one, do ask.

It's surprising how many authors fail to fill this form in – almost certainly because they are being asked for information that they have provided before. Take your time to fill it out and answer all the questions. Never just attach a CV and leave the person at the other end to sift through for the information they need. Even worse, please don't write (as I've witnessed): 'I've already told your editorial director, kindly consult him/her'. Remember that the marketing person dealing with your book will be dealing with lots of other titles simultaneously and if information about you and your book is difficult to find, they may give up the struggle. *This is a key promotional platform, so make the best possible use of it.*

Fill it out legibly – print or type rather than handwrite, and keep a copy. Be specific. Give precise details of conferences at which you will be speaking, the dates, venues and the organisers' contact numbers (fax, phone and e-mail). Don't just give the initials of societies – which will almost certainly mean nothing to someone not active in the field – and approximate dates.

# A & C Black
## Authors' Publicity Questionnaire

It will help us to promote sales of your book if you would fill in the answers to the following questions and send them to us as soon as possible. The information you give us will provide the basis of your book's promotion in the form of press releases, seasonal catalogues and leaflets, etc.

We appreciate that some of the questions may not be applicable to your book, so please do not feel bound by the exact wording of the questions and expand any answers on a separate sheet where necessary.

Please attach a recent black and white photograph of yourself.

| Book title (including subtitle) *Talking to Goldfish and listening to their answers* | Edition *1st* |
|---|---|

Author editor (if your name is ever mispronounced please indicate the correct pronunciation)
*Ambrosia Pheenne (pronouced Fin)*

Date of birth *12. 11. 57*    Nationality *Scottish*
(This information is required for some awards eligibility)

Address *23 Spottiswoode Close, Edinburgh*

Tel no. (home) _____
Tel no. (work) _____
Fax no. _____

*1* A brief biographical sketch including anything relevant to the writing of the book.
*A lifelong goldfish lover, I was inspired to write this book by my tenth goldfish Bertie. Having lost my job, I spent far more time in my flat than is usual and suddenly realised that he was consciously mouthing at me. I imitated his movements and conversation began. We have been communicating ever since. Neighbours were fascinated by the tale, it got passed on to our local paper, and I was persuaded that others would find this helpful. This book is the result.*

*2* Please list professional bodies, organisations, clubs, etc of which you are a member.
*I am a founder member of the Bruntsfield Acquatic Guild which has an extensive membership.*

*3* Have you published other books with us or other publishers? Please give titles, publishers, dates.
*Accounting for Beginners, A.B. Press 1987; More Accounting for Beginners, A.B. Press 1993; I have contributed many academic papers on accountancy for professional journals.*

4 Please write a short synopsis of your book (approx 150-200 words) including a summary of the contents which could form the basis of a book jacket blurb.

This is a complete guide on how to communicate with your goldfish. Humans and fish coexist but often take no notice of each other. This book provides step by step guidance on how to get the most out of the relationship. A fish's perspective on your life is absorbing and original - you would be suprised by what they notice - and your views on what it feels like to live out of water are equally interesting to them.

The book includes full guidance on mouth movements and appropriate accompanying noises to attract your fish's attention and ensure a two way dialogue.

5 For lack of space your book may sometimes have to be described in a sentence. What is the shortest statement you can make which aptly expresses its scope and theme?

Communicate with the goldfish in your life, in five easy stages.

6 Please list the main selling features of the book, who you hope will buy it and why.

This is a completely new book. To my knowledge no one else has written on the same subject. I find that the idea of talking to a fish appeals not only to all goldfish lovers, but also to those who have in the past thought of owning a fish but dismissed the idea as boring.

7 Are there any competing books? Please name them and explain how your book differs from them.

None. There was a professor in Lithuania who has given talks on the subject but he is now dead. No one is thought to have been passed his secrets before he died.

8 Are you willing to give press, radio and tv interviews? Yes

9 Would you be prepared to write (an) article(s) for the press on a subject related to the book? Yes

10 Have you any objection to your address or telephone number being given to media wishing to contact you direct? Yes, please vet all calls before passing them to me as some people have an unhealthy interest in communicating with fish.

*11* Is there any particular aspect of your book which may be of special interest to the media?

I think the whole thing is captivating.

*12* Have you any personal contact with people who might commend your book or promote the sales? (Media, librarians, booksellers, etc). Please give name, position, organisation address and telephone number where possible.

My sister is a librarian, a friend of mine runs a bookshop which would take copies. Contact details on the attached sheet. Animal Hospital should feature my book and Rolf Harris should be sent a personal copy. I am told that the former newsreader Martyn Lewis is fond of cats so may have a passing interest in how they relate to goldfish.

*13* Are there any regional, specialist or foreign publications to which you think review copies should be sent? Please give addresses where possible.

Edinburgh papers and broadcast media.

*14* Are there any areas or particular towns where local publicity and bookshop displays might be helpful? Please list these and give reasons.

I was born in Berwick upon Tweed and lived there until 10 years ago. Before that I lived in London.

*15* Do you ever make visits to schools, libraries, etc for book weeks?

I give talks in a local primary school during Book Week.

16 Can you suggest the names and addresses of societies or associations which might help to promote sales of the book, eg by undertaking the distribution of leaflets, or by supplying mailing lists or publishing a journal? Give a contact name where possible.

*I could include a flyer in the next mailing to members of the Bruntsfield Acquatic Guild as I am the secretary.*

17 Is there any particular season or event, to which you think publication should be linked? (conferences, exhibitions, etc)

*Most fish get bought in the autumn.*

18 Are there any academic, educational or professional institutions or courses that could use your book? Please give details including addresses where possible.

*I think my book should be recommended reading for all courses in veterinary medicine.*

19 Is the book of any special interest overseas? Which countries?

*Avoid countries where goldfish are eaten.*

20 Further suggestions

*Goldfish do not photograph well.*

Signature *Ambrosia Pheenne*          Date

## Writing copy for the book jacket

The copy that appears on the book jacket (commonly known as the blurb) may be drafted by the title's editor, or a freelance copywriter specialising in the writing of book jackets. It's also quite common for the author to be asked to write it.

### Case Study: *The perfect blurb*
I was about halfway through the writing of my book when I was asked to write a blurb for the back cover. I was quite surprised to be asked, but not displeased – the blurbs for previous books had been drafted by editors and I had never been totally satisfied with them.

The opportunity struck me as a highly significant one – here was my chance to sum up the value of the book, in a permanent format. This was all the more welcome because the book had been agreed upon so suddenly.

The book I was writing (a self-help book for a very specific market) had been commissioned very quickly. It had grown out of a chance meeting with the publisher, and as I am part of the market, and know exactly who I am writing for, it had taken me less than two days to draft a contents list and knock out an introduction and first chapter. And on this basis the book had been commissioned.

Since then I had been busy researching and writing the title, and uncovered a real need for the book I was writing. I felt passionately that the advice I was about to give would be well received, and very strongly that the group I was writing for were underrepresented and badly served by existing information sources.

I viewed the chance to write the book blurb as an opportunity to elevate the professionalism of the group I was writing for. I drafted a full page of closely argued text which I felt proud to have written and which colleagues were complimentary about. We all felt better about ourselves as a result.

Two days later I realised that what I had written was a manifesto for a possible professional association, not a book blurb, and of course I would have to start again.

## What a good book blurb should contain

A book blurb is there to entice a purchase, not justify a lifelong career or calling. Bear in mind that such blurbs are often read in crowded places particularly beloved of pickpockets, with shoppers jostling round you whilst your other purchases dangle from your other hand, and that books are often heavy and thus difficult to hold for a long time. It follows that there isn't time to take in lengthy copy.

A non-fiction book blurb should give a quick indication of who it is for and why they need it. A fiction blurb should both convey atmosphere and indicate what kind of book it is (mass-market or literary fiction). Quotes are extremely valuable to both fiction and non-fiction as they can pinpoint accurately what kind of expectations the reader should have.

I also think it's very important to match the words to the product. Do not make a romantic novel sound like an entry for the Booker prize: you will put off both potential markets.

## Case Study: An excellent blurb

Just before Christmas I was in Waterstones browsing for a title for a ten-year-old girl, who is not particularly keen on reading. The title shown caught my eye for the following reasons:

- very bright colour orange
- brilliant title. I knew the words 'thongs' and 'full frontal snogging' would get the intended recipient interested
- sample of the text on the back. She had really enjoyed Adrian Mole and this seemed to be equally funny
- rather pudgy looking adolescent on the front cover – she looks wholesome and unsophisticated
- very enthusiastic quotes from the *Sunday Telegraph* and the *Independent on Sunday* indicate that this is the purchase of a responsible adult – I have the girl's parents to consider
- front cover indication that the book won the Nestlé Smarties Prize in 1999 – i.e. it is considered an excellent read by the literary establishment.

In other words, this title effectively sold itself on two levels – both to me as an adult purchaser and to the person for whom it was bought, who read it very quickly and is now longing for the sequel.

## A meeting with your publisher to discuss marketing

Your contract will specify a date for delivery of the manuscript, and (usually) a planned publication date. About six months before publication it's a very good idea to get in touch with your editorial contact to talk about progress – by this stage the manuscript is most likely nearing the end of the editing process.

Even if it is not suggested, this is also the ideal time *to ask to meet* the marketing person who will be responsible for promoting your book.

## Some useful background tips for this meeting

Never assume that whatever information you have sent in about yourself and your book has either been circulated or fully read. Take another copy and mark the most important points.

---

This may sound like heresy, but many publishers make a conscious effort to cut down on what they have to read: there is simply too much of it. With manuscript submissions, strategy reports, CVs sent in speculatively by those wanting a job, in-house newsletters and many other documents competing for their attention, your information must stand out. So, use a highlighter pen to draw attention to key parts of your message, use cartoons, or paste on headlines from tabloid newspapers. *Above all, never forget that you are selling yourself to your publisher, long after they have agreed to publish your book.*

---

## The first meeting

(1) Smile and shake hands. Be positive and enthusiastic. Ask to meet all involved. You may be introduced to the head of the relevant section, but ask to meet those who will actually be doing the work on your book, irrespective of seniority. Ask for their business cards (most people have them but rarely get to hand them out) and remember their names when you call. Be warned too that publishing employees can rise very quickly – from marketing assistant to marketing director in as little as four or five years. If you insist on speaking only to the chief, you may be storing up resentment from someone who will very soon be important.

(2) Make no assumptions.

**You cannot assume that everyone you meet has read your book.**

Your editor is probably the only person you can rely on to have done so, and even then, the copy-editing will almost certainly have been done by someone else. It follows that all those who make decisions that affect the look of your book, and its marketing, need key information on what kind of title it is. The book jacket design and the blurb on the back of the book are generally agreed to be the two most important factors influencing purchase in bookshops. It is therefore very important that the person who is briefing the designer and the copywriter understands what they are writing about.

**The person responsible for marketing your book will not necessarily understand its subject matter**
Indeed, the more specialised the subject matter, the less likely this will be. Publishing attracts many more recruits with an arts background than a science background. For example, it's very common for high science titles to be handled by those with an arts background, and even those with relevant subject experience will often find themselves matched for their personality traits (for example, their ability to get on with difficult authors) or marketing/publishing skills rather than their relevant degree.

The marketing person's role is to understand who the market is, where to find them and how to approach them. But it doesn't follow that they start off with any background knowledge of that market. The best way for them to gain this is to ask you lots of questions, but don't assume that if they ask none they understand everything. They may be wary of admitting how little they know, and worry that if you knew this you might dismiss their ability to do the job – usually a mistake. When working on titles whose subject matter I know little or nothing about, I often find I do a better job as I am forced to think about who would buy it, rather than relying on my own out-of-date hunches based on inadequate knowledge.

**Not everyone you meet will have read your author publicity form**
Publishers are very bad at bureaucracy. If you are consulting your doctor, or dealing with your motor insurer, you can usually rely on every single piece of previous correspondence being with your file. Not so with publishers. Never assume that a let-

ter you sent has completed the circuit of all possibly interested/involved.

Take along a copy of the author publicity form to the meeting, and provide a list of bullet points updating those you meet on what you have been up to since. Remember that in addition to looking after your book, the marketing staff may have to come up with plans for 20–30 other titles during the same month, so if the information you provide is easy to use it is more likely to be acted upon.

### What to discuss at your first marketing meeting with the publisher

**What kind of title will this be?**
- Is this a key title (the jargon is 'lead title') or just one of the many they are publishing that season ('mid-list')? You will get a feel for this by the seniority of the staff involved in your meeting. (Titles that have passed their first peak of sales but, rather than going out of print, have passed into the house's standard list of titles available, are known as 'back list'.)
- How long is the payback period for the publisher's investment? How many do they intend to have sold by various points in the future (say three and six months, two and five years)? How long do they anticipate it will remain in print for? Do they anticipate a need to update it in a few years time? Is it part of a growing imprint or a completely new venture for them? You may be surprised to know that your contract with the publisher will very seldom include an indication of how many copies they are likely to print.
- What is the timing for publication, and is this of particular importance? In some areas of publishing, timing is absolutely crucial. A mass-market novel may have as little as six weeks in the shops before it is either reordered or sent back to the publishing house for a credit; children's titles may take years to get established. It follows that the timing of the marketing and publicity for books is particularly sensitive – the marketing must be timed to produce demand just at the time when the books are in the shops ready to be sold.

- Discuss how this overlaps with your own understanding of the market. Be realistic. Not every title will have national press advertising – it would be entirely counterproductive if it did. Talk about what you could do at the time of publication.

**How much money will be spent on marketing your book?**
Will the book be marketed on its own or in combination ('piggy-backed' or 'cooperatively') with other books from their list? Most publishers try to build a reputation as a particular kind of house with strengths in certain areas, so cooperative marketing is not necessarily a disadvantage if it means you reach more people by pooling the sums that might have been spent on titles individually.

**Is any direct marketing planned?**
Do you have any names and addresses you could contribute to the mailing lists? What societies do you belong to? Are their mailing lists available; could you get access to them at a special rate?

**What about promotional activity?**
Lots of magazines and newspapers feature 'reader offers' these days to boost loyalty. Can you think of any such media that might be particularly interested in your book? What other items do you buy on a regular basis that might make a useful link? For example, mail order catalogues sometimes use books to boost the size of the order. By organising promotions you may get space at a very competitive rate.

**What kind of marketing materials can be made available to you?**
Most authors can make use of leaflets on their books – perhaps to hand out if you are speaking or to give out at exhibitions? Could the publisher provide you with a showcard (a poster or notice on card, often made to stand up and with an appropriate backing like a photograph) to attract attention to the book when you are speaking?

Many authors who attend lectures, training seminars or conferences as a speaker take along stock to sell at the same time (or even get their book included in the price paid by delegates).

**SPECIAL OFFER**
only £3.99 with any order

SPEND £60 & RECEIVE
A £5 VOUCHER TO USE
ON YOUR NEXT ORDER

First Aid For Children Fast
Every household should have a copy.
See order form for full details.
*Ref* 5742                  Normal price **£9.99**
*Offer price* **£3.99** *with any purchase*
*(whilst stocks last)*

2    ORDER ONLINE www.JoJoMamanBebe.co.uk

**Books make good incentives for encouraging customers to order**

They can buy stock for this purpose from the publisher at a trade price (there is usually an extra discount if they buy in bulk) and thus make an additional sum to the royalty on each copy sold.

### What can you do to help?

Do you have an up-to-date photograph that could be used in publicity material? This does not need to be an expensive undertaking (find out when children in your local school are having their photographs taken and ask if you can be tagged on at either end of the day). Don't be bashful – a press release or leaflet will have seconds to make an impact; one that includes a photograph may attract more attention. Ensure the photograph has your name, the name of your book and your contact number on the back. Do you have contacts in the media and elsewhere that could be useful?

Do you have friends or colleagues that could provide a positive quotation about your book? An endorsement from a third

46

party will be much more valuable to the marketing team than the words they (or you) think up. Trawl through your address book for possible names and contact details to pass on to your publisher. Better still, approach them yourself and submit the details – if your contacts are famous it may be easier for you to approach them directly.

**Find out if the publishing house uses reps, and if so how they will be involved in selling your book**
Most publishing houses employ reps to either call on retail outlets, or at least phone them up on a regular basis. Are there local reps for your area (both where you live and work) that you could be put in touch with? For example, they might be able to organise a signing session or arrange PR in the local paper. Do you have contacts in the book trade (for example, a friend who runs a bookshop) who could be usefully mentioned to the local rep? Could you provide an interesting theme (or bit of gossip) about writing the book for your editor to pass on to the reps at the sales conference? Remember, as with so much marketing, the aim is to be memorable; to ensure the information sticks in the minds of those who make stocking decisions, as well as those who buy the end product.

## Final do's and don'ts

The don'ts first. I consulted many publishers whilst researching this book. Their comments on behaviour they found difficult in authors were almost unanimous. They disliked:

- rudeness. There are authors who demand the earth, but never bother to comment on anything that goes well
- unwillingness to get involved. 'I have already given this information to your editorial director, I suggest you contact him' is not very helpful if the latter is away and the information is needed urgently
- unrealistic ambitions. It is not possible to arrange mass-market advertising for books that will not sell in vast quantities. Of course, you could argue that mass-market advertising

might make them sell in that way, but would you risk your own money on such a speculative outcome?

But were really appreciative of those authors who do:

- think before they make a call. It's much better to consolidate your wish list into a single document and then arrange a meeting to discuss it, rather than constantly interrupting them as they try to get on with the business of marketing!
- allow enough time. If you need leaflets to reach the other end of the country for a speaking engagement, make sure you ask in plenty of time
- remain in touch. Send your contacts the occasional note of forthcoming key events and what might happen (for example, meetings at which you are speaking and at which information on your book could be handed out) and a note of thanks if things have gone well! This is not just good nature – you will be remembered, and if any additional opportunities come up (for example, 'filler' advertisements available at last-minute prices), maybe it will be your book that gets included.

# 6. Managing Without a Publisher: When to Go it Alone

I was recently in touch with an expert on porcelain who runs a highly successful retail business. He runs his shop from a delightfully rural address, advises the many customers who make a special visit just to come and see him, and writes well-researched articles for the associated specialist press.

This man had written a book on his particular expertise ten years ago, a title that had sold out, was now out of print, but for which there was a healthy demand in antiquarian bookshops. He had decided that now was the time for volume two. But with a strong personal reputation as a connoisseur, a loyal band of regular customers, an effective database for keeping in touch with them and the ability to take high quality photographs of the various artefacts that cross his threshold, all at his disposal, he had decided to manage the process himself this time. So rather than returning to the commercial publisher, he had decided to become his own publisher.

This is a very interesting example. With greater expertise in the subject matter than a commercial publisher could possibly bring to the project, and very strong contacts with the market likely to buy his book, he felt it was unreasonable to have to share the profits of the enterprise with those less able to contribute in equal measure. To supplement the operation, he planned to buy in expertise to cover areas he didn't know about (notably marketing and distribution).

Other authors decide to self-publish for much more personal reasons. Terence Frisby is a well-known playwright, with a string of published plays, including *There's a Girl in my Soup*, to his name. He also wrote the true story of a turbulent period in his life, *Outrageous Fortune*. The book dealt with a messy divorce, a battle over access to his son, the making and losing of a fortune, and lots of legal chicanery. The text was shown to a publishing house, and although interested, they produced 14 pages of notes on possible libel actions, all from eminent lawyers, that might result from publication.

Concluding that no professional publisher would take the risk, and because the book was important to him personally, he decided to go ahead and publish it on his own.

There are many similar examples of authors who decide to go it alone. This chapter is devoted to what you must consider if you are thinking of making a similar decision.

## Is there a market for the product you are considering?

Being passionate about porcelain is not enough to persuade everyone with a passing interest to part with money for your book. I was particularly impressed by this example because the author could identify precisely who would buy, already knew how to reach them, and expressed a genuine pleasure in matching market with product.

If you decide to publish yourself, you must be doubly sure of the answer to any question a commercial publisher would want to ask. And one of the first questions would be how large is the market and what proof is there that this is the case? If you are planning to publish the title yourself, you will be assuming the risk too, so your maths must be correct!

Secondly, you must enjoy the selling process. You must not feel demeaned by offering the product for sale yourself. I was interested to hear recently that part of the training process for new recruits to the insurance industry is to sell a product to a member of their own family or a friend, to overcome any initial squeamishness over the sales process. Terence Frisby commented:

> The author should never be embarrassed about asking for money for their book. I was quite resolute about this – after all, my friends know that the only time you get free seats in the theatre is when the show is no good. I was confident that the price was value for money for a good read in a high quality hardback binding.

My second line of argument in defence of the £16.95 price (£18 with postage) was that I had invested £10,000 of my own money in the project and so could not afford to give it away. I always offered potential customers the chance to have their book(s) signed for no additional cost, or even the chance to buy one of the rare unsigned copies!

My real disappointment was the retail book trade. I felt they were utterly apathetic when it came to selling my book. Time after time friends would report to me that they had tried to obtain my book in bookshops but had been informed by booksellers either that they had never heard of it, or that it would take 6 weeks to order from the publisher, when in fact it was on the database and could be obtained in 48 hours from the distributors, a well-known, reputable firm. This appalling attitude merely spurred me on to greater efforts. I sold lots as a result of after-lunch speaking engagements, book fairs and theatrical groups.

Out of a total print run of 2,000 I have sold over 1,500. I did not recover my costs (I never thought I would) but the project has brought me huge personal satisfaction.[1]

## What format should your product be?

Of course there are printers who can lay out and print a manuscript for you, but effective publishing involves far more than that.

The retail market today is obsessed by format. The impact of design and lifestyle programmes on television and features in the media has made us all much more style conscious than was the case even five years ago. Attractiveness of format now plays an increasing role in our decisions as consumers.

Commercial publishers have experience in choosing an appropriate format for each product under consideration. Sometimes,

[1] The book is *Outrageous Fortune*, available from First Thing Publications, 72 Bishops Mansions, Bishops Park Road, London SW6 6DZ, tel: 020 7736 2450. The title of Terence's publishing firm comes from a famous quotation from *Henry VI part II*: 'The first thing we do, let's kill all the lawyers'.

relatively minor product adaptations may make it accessible to a much wider market. For example, adding more illustrations or a more appealing cover may vastly increase a title's saleability. For professional books, aimed at a specific market, format considerations may be less important, and it may be effective just to match the format to an existing style. In the case of my porcelain expert, the main product considerations would be the quality of the photographs and the comprehensiveness of the volume's content. The size of the book is less important and could just be made to match other photographic compendia on the market.

If you feel that the style of the book you want to produce is a crucial part of its overall appeal, you may either decide to run with the professionals or employ the services of a book designer.

## Making the text easy to read: the role of the editor

Book editors face the difficulty that if well done, their job is absolutely invisible; the author's meaning shines through and the reader is never exposed to the stylistic problems that got in the way in the original manuscript.

The standard of editing in books published today is a subject raised relatively often in the media: there are frequent complaints of sloppy presentation and poor grammar making it through to the final product. Rather than viewing editing as a necessity, there are many cases in which editing is seen as a cost. Indeed, if the author's need for the publication is greater than the market's insistence on absolutely perfect text (for example, academic titles where to be published is essential to the professional reward system), authors regularly report that they are offered financial inducements to ensure the editing costs as little as possible. They may even be offered a financial incentive to deliver a 'pre-edited' text.

If you decide to publish yourself, it is almost certainly worth ensuring that what you say is easy to read, and you may consider employing the services of a professional editor. You can find one by contacting the Society of Freelance Editors and Proofreaders (see Useful Addresses).

Terence Frisby used a professional editing service (Amolibros:

see Useful Addresses) who also advised on production and marketing details, and helped him set up an agreement with a distributor. The porcelain expert is planning to do the same and has employed a former publisher to make appointments on his behalf.

## Marketing

Thinking about who to sell your book to should have been the very first stage in the decision to self-publish, and tackling this area should be high on your personal 'to do' list.

You will need various promotional items, depending on the market you are approaching, and a huge amount of motivation to see it through, whether or not you employ freelance help to organise the practical details.

### Information for bookshops/an advance notice
The basic promotional format of the book trade is an advance notice announcing a forthcoming title sent around 6–9 months pre-publication. See Chapter 4 for a sample. As you can see, it features all the basic information a retailer needs. Booksellers are selectable by specialisation (thus you can ask for a list of shops that specialise in children's books). You can get the addresses of booksellers and wholesalers from the Booksellers Association on sticky labels at a very reasonable price (see Useful Addresses).

### A press release
A press release will be needed to try to secure free publicity. See Chapter 7 for a guide on how to write one.

### A leaflet
The type of leaflet you need depends on how you plan to use it. Ideally it should be as multi-purpose as possible, capable of being sent to customers who enquire about your book, handed out at meetings, speaking engagements and exhibitions, and used to support a press release when sent to newspapers.

For copywriting hints, see Chapter 7.

### Sending out the book for feature or review

One of the most useful assets to anyone trying to achieve publicity for a new book is a string of contacts who can review or feature it in the media.

Authors are fortunate in that most newspapers and broadcast media have feature slots devoted to covering books – no other industry can rely on guaranteed space/coverage. What is more, the potential of both author and book can tickle the fancy of features editors as well as stimulate a story on the news pages – there are lots of opportunities for coverage. You may also become the subject of an in-house battle over space: different section editors like theirs to be the most popular.

The link between coverage in the media and boosted demand for the book is clearly established. Having said that, bear in mind that there are also lots of different publishers competing for this space, with over 100,000 new titles coming out every year in Britain alone. A publishing house will probably have access to one of the databases that keeps track of who is the relevant correspondent for each publication/programme. This is a very workable system and, with luck, a press release sent to the right person will result in coverage. If you are doing it yourself, you will need to be resourceful about finding out names and resolute in following them up. Here is some basic advice on putting together a list of contacts.

- **Never assume interest from anyone,** even if it's someone you have known since you were four years old. All contacts have to be worked at. Internal politics can ruin your chances – someone higher up the ladder may hate you; they may be jealous; consider you an upstart; lots of authors review books and you may have commented negatively on their sister's book and have thus generated ever-lasting dislike – writers can have very long memories.

  External forces can also drive you off the front page, for example war may break out.
- **Think about who might review your book.** The first names on your list will be easy (those you read yourself) but a great way to start building up a media contacts list is by reading and watching *other* media, in particular those you wouldn't

usually see. Media reading is a habit. We tend to read the papers we agree with, and as they confirm our prejudices, we can maintain a cosy idea that the world thinks as we do.

The *Sun* is easier to read than the broadsheets (and often better written), yet if you compare the readership of the tabloid with that of the same proprietor's *Times*, you will see the two papers' circulation figures are hugely different. Ironically, *Sun* readers account for a larger proportion of book buyers than readers of any other newspaper (because the circulation figure is so much higher, the percentage of regular bookbuyers is correspondingly larger).[1]

I was running a marketing course for ELT publishers recently and we were discussing which delegates read which newspapers. One commented that the *Daily Mail* is widely read by language teachers as the type of articles and language structure is ideal for ELT use. No one present admitted to ever reading this newspaper.

Look out for the names of relevant correspondents and in particular for reader offers – the kind where the journal provides editorial coverage of a product and readers can write in for a free copy. Most magazines will be happy to arrange such a deal – an editorial mention is far more influential than advertising copy, and also far cheaper.

- **Don't forget the local media.** Even if you never read the local press, don't assume everyone else does the same! Local radio stations and papers offer lots of opportunities for coverage of a local story. Crucially, they also offer practice in handling the media – for when you become a national celebrity! The approach taken is often much gentler than on the nationals, with the interviewer seeking to coax an interesting discussion, rather than ask questions you don't want to answer. What is more, many local radio stations are happy to run a short competition at the end of a feature, with listeners asked to phone in with the answers. This can substantially extend the coverage of your product, and consequently its memorability and eventual sale.

[1] Source: BML, *Books and the Consumer*, Market Research Report

Don't think local just means where you live. You may attract coverage where you grew up, used to live, or now work. Most local papers love a 'local boy/girl made good' story.

## How long should your list of contacts be?

Don't worry if your list is long – but don't send a free copy to everyone; if you do so you may erode the basic market of the book. Instead, circulate a press release with information on the book offering a free ('review') copy for those who offer to feature it. The more expensive the title, the more limited will be the review list, but journals may still announce publication even if they do not provide a detailed review.

Print off names and addresses and compile a card index for your desk. Make a note of what has been said after each call. Accuracy is essential; most people hate their name being misspelt.

## Achieving publicity and keeping your profile high

Have you noticed that certain politicians and 'television personalities' (whatever that means) are always being quoted. This is *not* because they sit at home waiting for the telephone to ring. It is usually because they have actively pursued notoriety: sent opinions to programmes which wanted sound-bites, and not been afraid to be controversial. In other words, they went in search of opportunities rather than waiting for them to find them!

Don't be intimidated by the idea of this. Remember that the very fact that you have a book being published implies determination (few authors are accepted by the first publishing house they approach), conviction (to have written a book in the first place) and self-confidence (why else would you assume that everyone wants to hear your opinion and that it deserves a wider audience). What is more, having written a book makes you interesting to the media – there is an assumption that if you are an author, you know something.

See Chapter 9 for ideas on raising your profile, both locally and nationally.

## Database management

An awareness of where the market is and how to approach it is the genesis of many a decision to self-publish, but be aware that database management of the information you hold is very time consuming and feels much less creative than the act of writing. This probably works best when the book is marketed to a customer database related to the subject of the book (for example, the porcelain expert mentioned above), but be aware that:

- managing a database takes time, immense attention to detail and constant updating
- you need to be aware of legal restrictions on the data you hold (see the Data Protection Act administered by the Data Protection Registrar (see Useful Addresses))
- you will need to invest in computer hardware on which to hold your contacts, software to make retrieving them possible, and explain to others how to extract information so that it can be done if you go under a bus
- data management must be an ongoing concern. For example, all the information you send out must have a return address so that 'gone aways' can be noted as such; you must be aware of duplication to avoid loading the same person more than once (very irritating and looks wasteful) but this is difficult to spot if people register themselves in their own and their maiden name, and use house names and numbers interchangeably. You may come to resent the time you have to spend on the database and thus cannot spend writing.

## Order fulfilment

If you do persuade customers to send you money for your books, who will fulfil these orders? Will having to pack up parcels get in the way of writing? Do you really want to spend your time packing parcels? Beware that books are easily damaged, heavy to post and high standards will be expected – no one wants to receive damaged books. As proof of this, watch customers choosing paperbacks in a bookshop – they may flick through a copy on display, but that will not be the one they take to the till point!

You may decide you want to appoint a distributor – look in the *Bookseller* for details of organisations offering such services, they run a feature on distribution and all those interested advertise. Be aware that:

- there are many more publishers wanting a decent distributor than organisations offering to be one
- you will have to pay heavily for the privilege, and pass on a percentage of sales made which have been secured through your efforts, not theirs
- you will probably deem it worth it if you get access to their rep force and they handle the areas you suddenly realise you know nothing about (for example, despatch of export orders and VAT).

Perhaps this chapter has made you realise there is more to being a publisher than is at first evident. An effective publisher brings to each author:

- experience
- confidence
- contacts.

You may decide it is preferable to get on with what you do best (writing), and delegate the above to the professionals. Alternatively, you may decide to go it alone. Whatever you decide, if the book is to be a success, *someone* must address the considerations listed at the very beginning of this chapter.

## Case Study 1: *Jane Tatam of Amolibros*

Jane Tatam who runs Amolibros has strong views about self-publishing. Having been in the publishing industry for over 20 years, she set up Amolibros with a view to helping authors self-publish, and providing professional assistance throughout that process. It seemed that the marketplace offered a choice of 'do-it-yourself – but not very well' or being ripped off by a vanity publisher, who would also give poor professional support for even more money.

She knows the industry well and hates the often snobbish attitude that both publishers and agents can have towards self-publishing. The self-publishing industry has been so beset by crooks, often called vanity publishers who feed on people's hopes and then disappoint them, that the result has been to blame those seeking self-publication rather than those who seek to defraud them. That is an enormous pity, because self-publishing has enormous potential. It represents the ultimate freedom of the press, and given the way many of the large publishing companies are now run, is a valid alternative for the discovery of new and exciting talent.

Even established authors turn to self-publishing from time to time. It is not a crime, nor a method of publishing to be derogatory about. (Called private publishing in the 19th century, it was once the respected pastime of the peerage.) It should be celebrated in much the same way as the Edinburgh Festival, and I believe eventually it could have a real place of merit, as an interesting and innovative fringe. If bad manuscripts are self-published, ultimately that doesn't matter – the industry proper is just as guilty of doing that. But every now and then, there may be a real gem, and for that it is really worth it. There is also enormous potential with informative and professional non-fiction writing, where knowledge of the marketplace can give the author a head start over the conventional publisher. Finally, as a method of archiving personal information, which may not be valued now, except within a limited marketplace, but could well be highly significant in years to come, not least for research purposes, it is invaluable.

Nobody should ever delude an author into believing it is easy to make a profitable success out of self-publishing – it certainly is not, particularly in the areas of fiction, poetry and memoirs, but it can be an enormously satisfying process. The sooner writers start thinking about marketing the better. It is best to realise from the outset that the majority of bookshops are unlikely to be supportive and are often prejudiced against self-publishing. Other ways must be sought, starting with pre-publication quotes from supportive worthies, and going on to designing direct mail campaigns, giving talks and offering to write articles. Even fiction can be sold this way, if the storyline has a solid 'peg' on which to hang the marketing. The internet is fast becoming a good way to sell books but its contribution should not be overestimated!

But every book that is self-published needs some loving care and professional attention to detail with regard to both the finished product and the marketing of it. That is exactly what Amolibros tries to provide. There is no handy formula for this – Amolibros gets to know its authors, helps them reach their objectives and provides a personal service coupled with professional expertise and a thorough knowledge of the industry and how it works.

For further information, phone or fax Jane Tatam on 01984 633713.

## Case Study 2: *Irene Lawford Music Publishing and Patronage, C.F. Peters: 1800 to the Holocaust*

Irene Lawford wanted to write the story of her family business, the music publisher C.F. Peters, which is hugely significant to both the history of music publishing and the role of Jews in the 19th and 20th centuries.

After 22 rejections over a substantial period of time (several publishers held onto the manuscript for months, or lost it, before deciding to reject it), she received an offer to publish. The firm, however, insisted that the manuscript be cut by a quarter whilst delaying the sending out of her contract (they insisted theirs was 'standard'). When she eventually delivered her cut manuscript, they returned a contract that professional advice described as draconian. Told that there was absolutely no opportunity to negotiate any of the content, she eventually suggested that she accept it all apart from the provision covering translation rights in Germany, where she felt there was a significant market. They refused any compromise whatsoever.

But having cut the manuscript herself, in preparation for publication, she decided that she now had a publishable product, and to proceed on her own. She used Amolibros to copyedit the text, typeset and supervise all aspects of publication. On their advice she appointed Gazelle as a distributor, and bought a book on marketing!

She had 2,000 copies printed. Perhaps with hindsight this was too many, but there were huge economies of scale that encouraged her to increase the order from the 1,000 she had at first envisaged. Reviews of the book were very good – she was featured in 12 journals, and this has been a very useful form of endorsement. The distributor has handled repping into bookshops and fulfilled trade orders.

Her main methods of sale have been direct marketing and personal initiative.

**Direct marketing.** She had 10,000 flyers printed, and mailed these to members of music societies and other organisations she belonged to – Anglo-German associations, the Hampstead Authors Society, Jewish groups; the leaflets even went out with her Christmas cards.

---

### MUSIC PUBLISHING AND PATRONAGE
### C.F. Peters: 1800 to the Holocaust
Irene Lawford-Hinrichsen
*With a Foreword by Yehudi Menuhin OM, KBE*

Publishing music requires intuition, sensitivity, patience and a love of music. It is an act of faith. It is also a business. This is the story of a business motivated by a concern for humanity. It tells of composers: their personalities, their conflicts and their music. It describes how music is published through the story of two men, Dr Max Abraham and Dr Henri Hinrichsen and reveals how they developed the small music publishing company: C. F. Peters Leipzig, to achieve world wide stature.

The book gives insight into the different aspects of music publishing. Quotations from correspondence illustrate the co-operation of the owners with the wider society. The company was founded in 1800 as Hoffmeister and Kühnel, Bureau de Musique, with the publication of music by Bach, Beethoven and Louis Spohr and was involved with the birth of copyright legislation. C.F. Peters himself, only owned it from 1814-1827.

1863 saw Dr Max Abraham's acquisition of the company, followed by his founding of the 'Edition Peters' and the Peters Music Library. A chapter covers his remarkable relationship with Edvard Grieg. The main thrust of the book is the period 1900 to 1940, when Abraham's nephew, Henri Hinrichsen became sole proprietor. He was, in due, course joined by his three eldest sons.

The complexities of society and politics are set side by side with the process of translating a composer's inspiration into sheet music and performance. The personalities and creativity of several composers and some musicologists are explored and the sponsorship of Edvard Grieg and Max Reger is emphasised. There is a detailed description of the traumas surrounding the publication of two major works - Schönberg's *Five Orchestral Pieces* and Mahler's Fifth Symphony.

Henri Hinrichsen was also a benefactor, patron of the arts and major supporter of Leipzig institutions. He was the founding benefactor of the first all women's college in Europe and he donated the Music Instruments Museum to Leipzig.

When the Nazis came to power in 1933, his and his family's world was destroyed. The Hinrichsens were Jewish and suffered the fate of so many under the brutal new laws enacted to deprive the Jews of all their rights and possessions. You can read the horrifying account of the confiscation and 'Aryanization' of C.F. Peters and the total marginalisation of Henri Hinrichsen who, in 1942, was gassed in Auschwitz.

C. F. Peters, Leipzig survived the Nazis, became GDR State owned and flourishes today in London, New York and Frankfurt. The final part of the book gives the fascinating background story to the creation of the three companies in the face of all the problems created by the Second World War. The 200th anniversary of the foundation of C.F. Peters is celebrated in December 2000.

356 pp. HB. 32 illustrations. ISBN 0-9536112-0-5. **Price £25.00 (US $50.00)**
Publication date: 3rd February, 2000. **Published by:**
**Edition Press, 22 Bouverie Gardens, Kenton, Middx. HA3 ORQ, England.**
E-mail: edition.press@btinternet.com Tel/Fax: 020 8907 2790

Available post free, payment with order, from the publisher.
(More information on our web site: www.btinternet.com/~irene.lawford/ )

---

Secondly, she gives as many related talks as possible, selling (signed) copies of the book afterwards. She writes to organisations that need occasional speakers and follows up leads provided by friends and acquaintances. Further leaflets are handed out on these occasions. She has written for magazines and journals about the process of self-publication, and her disillusionment with the publishing process, and this has led to both further interest in the book and in her as a potential speaker.

Of the 2,000 books printed, she sold 750 in the first year.

## Case Study 3: *Peter McHugh, Making it Big in Software*

Peter McHugh is a marketing consultant who wrote a book on how to grow a software company. He wrote a book largely to raise his profile in the industry, and his reasons for self-publishing rather than going through a publishing house were that he understood the market far better than any of the publishers he discussed the project with.

Publishers only talked about selling through bookshops and it was his conviction that this was not a bookstore book, but would sell far better direct to senior management in software companies. As in any such marketing push, the publishing house would be relying on him to do all the work, and he thought it better to handle the entire operation himself and avoid sharing the resulting profits.

Again he used Amolibros to edit the text. By trade standards (although not by business book standards) he set a relatively high price of £25, to cover the cost of direct marketing. He sold copies through mailing key management figures in software businesses, through extensive coverage in the computing press, through seminars and conferences at which he spoke, and from his website (offer price of £20 here). He placed a lot of emphasis on getting endorsements from recognisable names/firms in the industry, and this was very effective in persuading the market of the benefits of his book  The side benefit of the book for Peter was that he learnt about the publishing process at the same time – print and production, layout and graphics.

**MAKING IT BIG IN SOFTWARE**

*A guide to success for software vendors with growth ambitions*

PETER McHUGH

# Finally, the book which reveals ..... how to build a world leading software business from a small home market

*Making it Big in Software* is a practical guide to success for start-up and early stage software vendors with growth ambitions. For the current generation of software entrepreneurs, the book maps the route to world leadership by highlighting the lessons to be learnt from the experiences of established success stories. Throughout 250 pages in paperback format, it gives readers penetrating insights to the world of a fast-track software company.

### Learn from the successes and mistakes of the leaders

*Making it Big in Software* identifies the secrets of success by delving into the management ideas and strategies of leading UK software vendors. In-depth interviews with company founders (and key executives) illuminate the high growth process from start-up to IPO and beyond. Their experiences provide valuable insights into what's required to grow a world beater from the UK.

Just as important, their anecdotes profile the many potential trapdoors and blind alleys along the route to success. This one-of-a-kind book transfers 'best business practice' from proven role models to early stage software vendors.

### Blend the ingredients for success into a winning formula

*Making it Big in Software* provides a framework for managing a fast growth software business, built around the distilled wisdom of those who've done it. The book details the factors underpinning successful start-ups from creating a customer-centric product and a balanced management team to securing equity funding and undertaking an IPO. Furthermore, it delivers valuable guidance on formulating and executing a winning business model, incorporating advice on forming effective partnerships and indirect sales channels. And crucially, it defines the success criteria in building a thriving export business, dealing particularly with the difficult process of going to America.

*Making it Big in Software* reveals the required business strategies for success at each key stage of company development. And in the final chapter, it consolidates the criteria for success into pragmatic Action Agendas catering for companies at different points in their life cycle.

| Companies profiled |
| --- |
| Antonomy |
| Cadcentre |
| CBT Systems |
| Cedar Group |
| CODA |
| Dr Solomon's |
| Gentia Software |
| Iona Technologies |
| JBA Holdings |
| Kewill Systems |
| LondonBridge Software |
| Quality Software Products |
| Rolfe & Nolan |
| royalblue Technologies |
| Sage Group |
| Select Software Tools |
| Sherwood International |
| Smallworld |
| Staffware |
| Systems Union |
| Tetra |
| Zergo |

### For the first time, a book written in the UK... for UK software companies

**A two-sided leaflet sent to potential customers**

## What they're saying about Making it Big in Software

"Peter McHugh is to be congratulated for his thorough review of the factors involved in growing a successful global software business from the UK. I admire the attention to detail of his guide which is both interesting and an invaluable point of reference for the software industry."

John Pemberton — CEO, *Systems Union*

"For any UK software company looking to grow its business, this is the most relevant and pragmatic guide which I have read".

Gordon Crawford – CEO, *London Bridge Software*

"Must be read by any aspiring start-up that wishes to operate world-wide, especially in the USA".

Paul Rolph — *Chairman, Gentia Software*

"Peter McHugh should be congratulated. This fine book joins 'Crossing the Chasm' as essential reading for anybody wishing to build a successful software company."

Crispin Gray — *CEO, CADCENTRE*

"Should be on every aspiring software executive's bookshelf".

Alan Vickery — Chairman, *JBA Holdings*

"I went looking for a book like this when we embarked on our product strategy and didn't find one - shame Peter didn't write it six years ago"

John Hamer — CEO, *royalblue Technologies*

"… an excellent companion for the software entrepreneur. This book will play a vital role for those looking to reduce the learning curve, and get to market fast."

Colin Newman — VP, *IONA Technologies*

"…. entertainingly written, full of useful information and really interesting stories. "

Pamela Gray — President, *ISV Inc*

"A most worthwhile enterprise which I recommend to would-be new entrepreneurs, as well as those already engaged, in the software business".

Malcolm Rolfe — Founder, *Rolfe & Nolan*

### The Author

Peter McHugh established RUBIC, a software-specific strategy consultancy, in 1991. Since then, he has assisted nearly 100 software companies with all aspects of growth and export development. Prior to founding RUBIC, Peter worked in venture capital and management consulting. He holds degrees in Engineering and Management Studies.

### Written for…..

- Executives considering a software start-up.
- Early stage software entrepreneurs looking to move into high growth.
- The investment community looking to better understand the needs of a growing software company.

**For a detailed description of the book's content, as well as purchase information…… visit    www.makingitbig.net**

**Alternatively, use the enclosed order form to buy the book.**

**Testimonials are a very effective way of presenting a message**

*August 25th 1999*

---

**Announcing a new SOFTWARE BUSINESS BOOK**

## *Making it Big in Software* ..... the book which reveals how to build a world leading software business from the UK

*Making it Big in Software* is a practical guide to success for start-up and early-stage software vendors with growth ambitions. This is the first book which addresses the specific issues and challenges facing UK software companies; most books of this genre are written for an American audience. For the current generation of UK software entrepreneurs, the book maps the route to world leadership by highlighting the lessons to be learnt from the experiences of established success stories.

John Pemberton, founder and CEO of accounting vendor *Systems Union* commented, "Peter McHugh is to be congratulated for his thorough review of the factors involved in growing a successful global software business from the UK. [It is] an invaluable point of reference for the software industry."

*Making it Big in Software* is written both for executives considering a software start-up and for early-stage software entrepreneurs looking to move into a high growth phase. It will also be of value to those in the investment community looking to better understand the realities of life in a growing software company.

### Highlights the lessons to be learnt from the UK's leading lights

*Making it Big in Software* identifies the secrets of software success by delving into the management ideas and strategies of over 25 leading UK software vendors such as Sage, Dr Solomon's, JBA and London Bridge Software (the fifth best performing of all shares on the London Stock Exchange during 1998). In-depth interviews with company founders (and key executives) illuminate the software lifecycle from start-up to IPO and beyond. Their experiences provide penetrating insights into what's required to grow a world beater from the UK. Just as important, their anecdotes profile the many potential trapdoors and blind

**Press release: the copy could easily be used whole by journalists; subheadings and lists vary the pace**

alleys along the route to success. The intention is to transfer 'best business practice' from proven role models to early-stage software vendors.

## Blends the ingredients for success into a winning formula

*Making it Big in Software* reveals the five fundamental business strategies which differentiate the leading UK software vendors from the mediocre players:

1. Creating a customer-centric product.
2. Nurturing a balanced management team.
3. Securing equity finance to fund growth
4. Formulating and executing a winning business model.
5. Charting a route to export markets.

The book provides a framework for managing a fast growth software business, built around the distilled wisdom of those who've done it. It provides practical advice on forming effective strategic partnerships and indirect sales channels. And crucially, it outlines how to build a thriving export business, dealing particularly with the difficult process of going to America. The final chapter consolidates the criteria for success into pragmatic Action Agendas catering for companies at different points in their lifecycle.

Crispin Gray, Chairman of Cambridge-based *CADCENTRE* concluded, "This fine book joins *Crossing the Chasm* as essential reading for anybody wishing to build a successful software company."

## About the Author

Peter McHugh established RUBIC Consulting in May 1991 to specialise in strategy and marketing services for early-stage software vendors. Since then, RUBIC has worked with nearly 100 companies on all aspects of building a successful software business, in particular growing an export revenue stream. Prior to founding RUBIC, Peter worked as a venture capitalist and management consultant.

Peter graduated from University College Dublin with an Honours degree in Chemical Engineering in 1984 and has since completed a number of post graduate Management courses.

For a REVIEW COPY, further information, or interviews contact...
RUBIC Publishing, Grosvenor House, 25 St Peter Street, Tiverton,
DEVON EX16 6NW
Tel: (01884) 251 288                    email: mibis @ rubic.demon.co.uk

Published by *RUBIC PUBLISHING* (distributed by Gazelle Book Services)
Price £20                    ISBN 0-9535487-0-8
Publication date: Thursday 19th August 1999

*For a detailed description of the book's content and listing of the
companies profiled in the book......*
*visit          www.rubic.co.uk*

# 7. Writing Promotional Materials: How to Get Noticed

This section deals with various forms of written communication – all designed to get across the message that your book is worth taking notice of. You may not have to write this sort of information – most publishing houses prefer to do it themselves unless the subject matter is particularly specialised – but you may well be asked to check it. It follows that guidance on what kind of words to use, and when, will be useful.

I'll start with some specific guidelines for writing promotional copy, then proceed to give hints on the most common promotional formats and how to write for them.

## What is promotional copy?

Promotional copy consists of words that aim to sell.

It is not the same as writing an essay, or a memo to explain a proposition. You should always remember that the reader of promotional copy has a choice, to read or not to read, and consequently you must make it as easy as possible for them to absorb what you have to say. In achieving this, your most useful asset is a grasp of selectivity.

For example, you may be able to think of 20 reasons why a potential reader should buy your book, but you should probably restrict yourself to two or three; perhaps even just one, depending on the time and inclination of the market to listen to you.

### Think first about the audience

Your starting point should always be to concentrate on the audience to whom you are writing. What kind of people are they; reading your material in what kind of circumstances? How much time do they have to read? What else did they receive in the same post? How interested are they in what you are describing? If you adopt this approach, your material is far more likely to be appropriate and hence be read.

The needs and priorities of your audience must be uppermost in your mind all the time. Talk about what interests them and how your product meets their needs. Describe the advantages and benefits of your book, rather than its features. For example, instead of: 'This book includes a chapter on marital therapy', consider: 'A valuable chapter on marital therapy allows you to try out the techniques top consultants recommend'.

A good way of finding out whether your copy is sufficiently benefit laden is to add the phrase: 'which means that. . . ' to the end of every product feature you describe. For example: '200 top cooking tips included' would become '200 top cooking tips included which means that you can start saving time in the kitchen immediately'.

## Keep it simple

There is a temptation to dress up explanatory copy in long words, in an attempt to really convince the market that a purchase will be money well spent.

When writing promotional copy, however, it is usually far more effective to concentrate on simple benefits and promises, which can be grasped immediately. For example, instead of: 'A detailed explanation of marketing techniques that have been developed and practised over Mr Stockbridge's entire career in British manufacturing', consider: 'Here is the wisdom gained from a lifetime's experience in British industry'.

Along the same lines, try to write in the present tense, using words you are familiar with yourself (rather than ones that are part of your 'reading' vocabulary – words you understand but do not use in speech very often). A useful method of finding out whether your text is easy to read or not is to read it out loud. If you stumble over particular words or phrases, or cannot reach the end of the sentence without needing to pause for breath, the odds are that the text is difficult to read.

The words you use should be immediate in their impact, and are more likely to be of Saxon origin, rather than Latin. For example:

| Saxon | Latin |
|-------|-------|
| news  | information |
| now   | immediately |
| hurt  | injured |
| eaten | digested |

In addition, try to use terms that are vivid rather than hackneyed, for example:

| Vivid | Hackneyed |
|-------|-----------|
| love  | like |
| hate  | dislike |
| adore | love |
| deranged | mad |

Be very careful in the number of adjectives that you use. Try not to be over-regular, for example, giving every noun two adjectives which can get very boring:

> This useful and timely book. . .
> This current and up-to-date title. . .
> This accessible and readable manual...

One, none, or perhaps three might be more effective.

Asking questions is a good way of involving the reader, provided they are not questions which attract a swift no and a jettisoning of the promotional piece!

Link the sentences and paragraphs using easy to read phrases like:

> It follows that. . .
> This means that. . .
> In this way you can see how. . .

Having said keep the text simple, the insertion of interesting and unusual words can be extremely effective, if they are surrounded by simpler terms. For example:

> There was nothing to commend him but his smile. And

she was surely too old, and had too much common
sense, to be beguiled by a smile.

The use of 'commend' and 'beguiled' lend an intriguing
aspect to this cover blurb for a historical novel.

For interesting words, use a thesaurus on a regular basis,
and try to read good English – subscribe to *The Spectator*!

## Match your vocabulary to the market

Promotional materials supporting a title should be written in a
style that is appropriate to the book. Do not make a beach read
sound like a Booker prize-winner, or a basic 'how to' book
sound like an Open University textbook. People make very
quick decisions on the basis of the copy you present.

They will also be very wary of buying from you a second
time if they feel they have been misled the first. If they buy a
book from you on the basis of copy and your product does not
live up to the expectations generated, their disappointment will
be remembered. This is particularly difficult if you are seeking
to develop a brand image for yourself or the publishing house.

Be very wary of jargon, or 'professional' speak. Many special interest groups, whether bound together through work or
pleasure, develop an accompanying vocabulary. Such 'jargon'
serves to make those who belong feel a part of it, and those
who do not outsiders, but such words are dangerous in promotional copy. Why?

Firstly, because jargon changes all the time, so you can
appear out-of-date very quickly, particularly if your promotional material will have a long life on someone else's shelves.
Secondly, you are in danger of getting it wrong and making
your promotional piece look out of touch or even ridiculous.

On the other hand, there may be certain buzz words that
you need to use to show to the market that this is a particular
kind of title, for example: 'textbook', 'reference title', 'saga',
'bedtime story'.

Pay particular attention to issues which may offend your
market, and make no assumptions about it. Never assume all
firemen are male or all nurses female. You will annoy those
who are sensitive and everyone else will be aware of the gaffe.

Aim for a tone that is reasonable and hard to disagree with rather than one of academic argument refuting any suggestion that a title is not needed. Clichés and puns can be useful for making a sales proposition seem familiar, but I tend to avoid outright humour.

### Endorsements are enormously useful

The publisher (whether yourself or a company) is expected to say that a book is worth reading. Far more persuasive is the opinion of an objective outsider. This could be in the form of an extract from a review (but of course a first edition will not have access to reviews until after publication).

So, if you are a first-time author, or your book is a departure from your usual kind of work, think carefully about who you could get to endorse what you have written. Go through your address book and think about the past – who do you know who could give you a useful plug? If your book has particular relevance to a subject that is currently very topical, is there someone whose opinion would be influential if it appeared on the book jacket?

Asking for endorsements is not as difficult as you might think. In general, many people like to be helpful, and the resulting publicity may serve their own ends. On occasion you may be asked to draft the kind of thing you would like them to say. This may be because they are short of time, or because they want to ensure they write something appropriate. Whatever the reason, it's a wonderful chance to write your own review.

If you have no endorsements or quotes, are there official publications that you can quote? These may have nothing to do with your specific publication, but if they prove the need for the product, or give the storyline validity, they may be considered relevant. For example, a novel based on medical incompetence could benefit from being promoted in conjunction with news coverage of hospital staff shortages or recent medical disciplinary cases.

Wherever possible, break down the statistic into the personal. For example, instead of: 'Last year there were 850,000 cases of medical negligence', how about: '10 per cent of hospital admissions result in a case of medical negligence' or: 'If you are admitted to hospital, you have a one in ten chance of something going wrong'.

### *Effective design makes copy easy to read – and act upon*

As you write, think about how the text will appear as a pattern on the page. The key thing to look out for – and avoid – is predictability. Always remember that writing promotional copy is very different from writing essays; formulaic writing that is suitable for work that has to be read in order to be assessed will not do here. An introduction, three or four dense paragraphs of copy, all of roughly the same length and number of sentences, followed by a conclusion, will most likely not engage the reader's attention. Essays *have* to be read in order to be marked – readers of promotional copy have a choice.

Dense copy is off-putting, so break it up using bullet points, short paragraphs and subheadings. Try to vary the length of both sentences and paragraphs so that the overall effect is enticing.

Keep the measure of the text (the width over which the text is spread, from left to right) on the narrow side, so that it can be read easily. (Think how easy it is to read down the centre of a newspaper column, absorbing the message without reading every word. This is because the measure is narrow.) Wide text measures tire the eye, and tired eyes stop reading. The same goes for other design techniques, which serve well in small quantities to attract attention, but can be very wearing if overused. For example:

- using too many CAPITAL LETTERS
- reversing large amounts of solid text out of a colour (out of a photograph is even worse)
- justifying text so that the blocks of copy appear solid
- fitting text around photographs and illustrations so you end up with a ragged left-hand margin
- making the typeface very small or very large
- using too many typefaces
- using clashing colours, for example bright blue on a bright red background

All of the above can work well when used in small quantities to attract attention, but have the opposite effect when over-used. They make the words difficult to read.

## Press releases

A press release is an information sheet sent to a journalist to try to stimulate media coverage. This is usually achieved in one of two ways:

- the journalist uses your press release in its entirety, inserting the words you supply into the paper/medium they write for
- the journalist decides to write/commission a feature based on the information you send in – usually an author interview or an article on the issues your book draws attention to.

The main point to bear in mind is that most journalists receive hundreds of press releases every day; the more desirable the medium you are pursuing, the more press releases they will receive. The best advice is to:

- keep it short (a single side of A4 is plenty)
- divide up the copy with subheadings and into short para-graphs so that it is easy to read
- make it interesting.

The latter is easier said than done. To start with, cut out long sentences of introductory copy about the publishing house and background information on the author (unless strictly rele-vant). Try to bring the atmosphere of the book to life, or to highlight the issues it raises, rather than give a complete account of the content.

For example, is Daphne du Maurier's *Rebecca* a compelling tale of one woman's jealousy for a dead rival, or the story of a local landowner's second marriage to a much younger woman?

Bear in mind too that the publication of yet another book is not really news to a journalist – there will be at least 400 other titles published the same day! What the journalist wants is a story, so what kind of 'peg' on which to hang one can you offer? This may be something in the book, but equally could be something in your background, or in the news, or a publicity event tied to publication.

Other facts to bear in mind when preparing press releases:

- give your press release a headline, not just the book title. A headline serves to draw the eye in, it does not need to be a complete summary of what follows
- put the main facts in the first paragraph (the journalist may get no further). Harold Evans, former editor of *The Times* said that the first paragraph of a press release should include the 'who, what, where, why and when'.
- if you are trying to get feature coverage, try to make the press release specific. For example, the *Daily Mail* would be interested in a different angle from the *Financial Times*, although both could cover the same book
- if the journalist does decide to use the whole press release, it will be cut from the bottom upwards, so start with the most interesting/significant information, and develop themes further down the page
- ensure your grammar is correct, particularly when writing to literary editors. You are writing to people who care about words and if the press release is poorly compiled your readers will assume the book is of the same standard
- do not repeat the book jacket copy in the press release. This looks lazy and is wasting a separate opportunity to communicate with the market
- always put a contact name and number at the bottom of the page (it could be someone in the publisher's publicity department or perhaps your own). If you are available for interview or some other possible feature (for example, you could give a demonstration based on the subject of your book, or provide questions for a basic competition) then the press release should say so
- try to make the press release visually arresting. Can you include illustrations – perhaps cartoons, an author photograph or an illustration from the book? In a further bid to make your release stand out, can you print the release on coloured paper? If 99 per cent of the postbag is printed in

black ink on white paper, a coloured sheet will draw attention to itself

- be wary of using quotations on press releases. If you do, it must be clear that they draw attention to the book's great interest and don't imply that every angle has already been thought of. For this reason, at the end of quotations on a press release provide the names of the contributors rather than the media in which they have appeared.
- don't send press releases out too often or if you don't have particular news to impart. You will devalue your future impact. What is news? Peter Hobday provided this useful litmus test:

  Something that is unusual enough to be noticed so that the reader will want to talk about it to his wife at home or in his local with his mates.[1]

[1]*Managing the Message*, Peter Hobday, Allison and Busby

**A&C BLACK**

A&C Black (Publishers) Limited · 35 Bedford Row · London WC1R 4JH
*telephone:* 020 7242 0946  *fax:* 020 7831 8478  *email:* enquiries@acblack.co.uk

May 2000

Dear SEN Coordinator

### Do you know about Graffix?

Whether you are already familiar with the series, or this is the first time you have heard of them, here is your chance to <u>order at a discount</u> (if you order before the end of half term).

**Graffix are books in comic format.** They are full of interest and ideal for reluctant readers (in particular boys). The short chapters and compelling story lines make them very motivating to read. First launched three years ago, the series has grown in popularity very quickly - mainly through word of mouth. There are now 30 titles to choose from.

The enclosed leaflet gives you more information and a full list of all the books in the series but there are a couple of points that I would like to emphasise now:

### 1. Graffix offer you compelling stories for reluctant readers - who don't like being patronised!

A quick glance through the list of books available will show you why Graffix are so popular. Titles like *Goal Getter, Headless Ghost, Horror of the Heights, Girl Gang, Haunted Surfboard* jump off the shelf and attract attention.

Our feedback has been that both the pupils and the Learning Access Team love these books. The illustrations are instantly compelling and the short chapters motivating to read. Readers get a real sense of progress.

> "At last! Books to encourage the reluctant older reader. The appeal is instant and the content spot on - with loads of street cred."
>
> ***Andrew Cullum**, Head of Year (CURRENTLY KEY STAGE 3)*

Indeed, several of the books in the series have been written for us by authors who write for us in another capacity - <u>because as parents of reluctant readers they wanted to be part of a new series that really does get children reading.</u>

> "The vocabulary is accessible but also challenges and extends. The high quality comic illustrations really support the text. A great addition to our SEN library."
>
> ***Anita Miles**, SEN Teacher (SECONDARY)*

*Chairman and Joint Managing Director* **Charles Black** *Joint Managing Director* **Jill Coleman**
*Directors* **Paul Langridge · Terry Rouelett · Janet Murphy · Oscar Heini · Robert Kirk · Susan Kodicek**
*Registered Office* **35 Bedford Row London WC1R 4JH England · Regd no 189153**
*Distribution Centre* **Howard Road Eaton Socon Huntingdon Cambs PE19 3EZ** *telephone:* **01480 212 666** *fax:* **01480 405 014**

**Copy for a direct mail letter. Note how the reader's attention is drawn to key points of the text by using design effects such as indenting, bold and underlining**

**2. Stories that are well plotted and convincing - just in comic format!**

Before a book idea is turned into a Graffix, it has to be a winner in its own right. Our editorial team pick stories from authors who like to write for this age-group (11+), and then turn them into the Graffix format - working with an illustrator and specialist editor to divide up the text.

This means that all the usual devices of effective story-telling - like a strong opening, suspense, character development and so on - are there. The books are ideal for literacy work, as the basis for discussion and paired or group reading sessions.

So, just because the book appears as a comic does not mean there has been any compromise in the quality of the story telling.

**Try Graffix out and save money as you do so**

The best way to experience Graffix is to try them out with your reluctant readers. We'd like to offer you the chance to do just that with our special 'six books for the price of five' offer. All you have to do is mark your selection on the enclosed order form, and return to the address shown. Alternatively you can phone or fax us an order. We will even pay the postage for sending you the books you order. All orders must however be received by the end of half term.

So, please do give Graffix a try. With our special offer you have nothing to lose, and your reluctant readers everything to gain!

Yours sincerely,

*Kate Petty*

Kate Petty, Graffix Editor

P.S. There is no limit to the number of titles you can order, but to get the maximum number of free books your order must be a multiple of six and returned by the end of half term. If you order all hardback titles your sixth book will also be a hardback.

**If you are writing to a market that you suspect may be resistant to being 'marketed' to, it's a good idea to have the letter signed by someone else, in this case an editor**

## Catalogues and websites

Most publishers produce an annual catalogue and seasonal lists announcing their forthcoming wares. Many also have a website on which author and title information is displayed. The most important point to remember when checking copy for use here is that it will be presenting:

- the list as a whole. The books will appear side by side so it's important not to use the same words, or selling point, for each title
- it must be comprehensible to people who are not subject specialists but nevertheless have the power to circulate information to those they know might be interested (for example, librarians, booksellers, reps, those opening the post). It's always dangerous to assume that because author and editor understand the copy, and the end user will too, that no one else matters!

## Point of sale materials

These are promotional materials displayed where books are paid for, such as boxes to hold large quantities of stock (usually called dump bins), bookmarks, balloons and posters. Their chief function is to remind the potential purchaser to buy, and so the words used on them must be both interesting and legible (preferably from the other side of the shop!).

There is huge scope for producing low-cost point of sale materials that nevertheless have a great impact on the market's willingness to buy. What is more, as the producers of ink on paper, publishers have an ability to create such things much more cost effectively than other manufacturers. The following can all be produced relatively cheaply:

- postcards for handing out at the till
- bookmarks, using the cover artwork
- badges (particularly good for children's titles)
- balloons

- showcards
- shelf wobblers (T-shaped piece of card that sits beneath the books on a shelf and protrudes to attract attention)
- posters.

## Writing mailshots

Writing direct marketing materials is a very specific art, but mastery here will help you when writing many other promotional pieces. The basic principles are:

- you must provide enough information to enable the customer to make a buying decision. Any question that a customer could answer by looking at the product in a bookshop must be addressed. This includes size, format, number of illustrations, how the information included was put together, binding, and so on.
- repeat yourself. No mailshot is read from start to finish. Readers tend to dip in and out. It follows that the key selling points must be repeated so that they are not missed, although not using the same words each time. Someone once laid down the theory of writing a mailshot as:
  tell them what you are going to tell them
  then tell them
  then tell them what you have just told them

- divide up the information so that it is easy to read. Space is what draws the eye in to read further, not densely packed text
- start reading your own direct mail and look out for the best examples. I'll hazard a guess that the best ones are those that make a reasonable case for the product being sold, and explain why it is needed, rather than those that dazzle with flashes and colours
- most mailshots consist of four things: a brochure, a letter, a response device of some sort and an outer envelope. The letter is the most highly read part of the mailshot because it looks the most personal

81

Lastly, whatever kind of promotional material you are working on, don't forget to check that the following information is both present and up-to-date, so that ordering is easy:

- author name (spelt correctly; do double check)
- book title (ensure the most up-to-date title is listed, not the working title)
- publisher name, address and contact numbers
- ISBN (every book has a different International Standard Book Number)
- price (ensure it is up-to-date)
- publication date (ditto)

With this information any book can be ordered from any bookseller, usually at no extra charge (although a small deposit may be required). This is often forgotten by customers, who assume that because other industries don't work this way, it is not possible to order a single copy of a book (in food terms you would have to order an 'outer' with 24 or 48 lots). I think it's worth reminding customers!

# 8. How to Get Publicity

What is publicity? You will probably have noticed that marketing terminology is used very casually in publishing. In some companies 'publicity' is a catch-all phrase for marketing activity or staff; in others it may be the specific job of one person.

In the context of this chapter I am talking about publicity as editorial coverage in the media which leads to both promotion by word of mouth and sales. Publicity is often a subliminal sell; the publicist tries to lodge so many references to a particular project in the brain of the consumer that the latter is prompted to buy the book without ever having formally made the decision so to do.

An important point to grasp is that because publicity strives to achieve editorial space, i.e. to get your project included in a newspaper's features or news coverage rather than as a paid-for ad, the publicist is effectively asking for something for nothing. At the same time, all media can calculate exactly what the space is worth (from their advertising rates). It follows that in return for the space allocated, the medium chosen will certainly want something in return: a scoop (a story before anyone else has it) or an interesting angle that will appeal to their readers. However, the story they want to feature and the image you want to present may not be the same.

You should also remember that:

- publicity should communicate with the target market for the title you are promoting, and not be an end in itself
- publicity is not the same thing as public relations; achieving publicity does not always mean gaining positive coverage. A negative story may generate interest and sales even more effectively than a positive one

- publicity must be accompanied by information on availability (where and how) for sales to result.

## How will publicity be orchestrated

Most publishing houses have a publicity department. It does not follow, however, that all authors and books get publicity organised on their behalf. The author who suggests angles that could be exploited, media vehicles to be pursued, and is cooperative in the process, is more likely to obtain the attention of the house publicist. Remember that in any single month it is likely that your publishing house will be promoting at least 30 titles. There is not enough time, energy or resources to go round.

## Dramatis Personae – publicists and journalists

Publicists deal with journalists. They try to persuade them to cover the author/book they are promoting. They are either working for the house that is publishing the book, or may be working as a hired hand, perhaps employed by a firm of publicity specialists or as a freelance.

It may help you to get the most out of both publicists and journalists if you know what kind of people you are dealing with. Characteristically (and this is a generalisation), publicists are:

- eternal optimists – they keep going when rejected
- good at juggling – they have to deal with lots of different ideas at different stages of development at the same time, and remember which one is at which stage
- perhaps less interested in your literary skills than in your ability to attract headlines. Bear in mind that by the time a publicist gets involved, the book has already been commissioned; their professionalism lies in making the media sit up and take notice, not in literary appreciation. So don't be dispirited if they make little reference to your book's merit and concentrate only on its news potential.

If the book is really strong in its own right (great read, won a significant literary prize, first novel that has huge potential) they may be able to generate coverage on its own merits, but even then the accompanying story will be relevant (think of Zadie Smith and Arundhati Roy – both hailed as wonderful novelists but their looks and personalities still very much used in the publicity process).

Again, these are generalisations, but journalists are:

- cynical – they have seen it all before; it's up to the publicist to tempt them with new ideas
- busy – and with their time at a premium, the more you can do for them, the better (from your point of view) the likely end results. Press releases written in a way that allows a specific journalist to incorporate them immediately will always do better than those made for blanket application
- distracted – they work in offices where most of us would find it very difficult to concentrate: phones ring, people talk loudly
- overwhelmed by other people's information: a realisation of just how many press releases a journalist or literary editor gets each day can be very dispiriting
- according to Dotti Irving of Colman Getty, more inclined to believe each other than the publicist, which is why a feature in a national newspaper can sometimes encourage other nationals to pick it up
- increasingly well-known in their own right:

> The relationship between interviewer and interviewee has changed over the same period [the last 40 years – since he began writing]. What used to be a rather bland and deferential conversation has become more probing and aggressive. Interviewers want blood – the blood of new and personal revelations – in exchange for the free publicity they offer their subjects. They want to assert their own personalities, and to demonstrate their own literary skills. They can become minor celebrities themselves in consequence. The interviewees, on the other hand, are apt to feel wounded and betrayed by such treatment.
>
> David Lodge, afterword to *Home Truths*, Penguin

## What an author can do to help in the publicity process

### Be helpful
Accept that publicity is going to help sell the book. Decide to cooperate even though personal coverage in mass media is not to your taste. Be prepared to be resourceful about what you have done in the past; the publicist will want you to be as unsqueamish as you can about others digging into it.

### Be pro-active
Provide a list of your useful contacts, experiences, future plans, and so on.

### Keep in touch
Let your publicist know what you are up to – all snippets of information can be useful. For example, if you are asked to judge a literary prize, or awarded a directorship, your publicist may be able to sell a feature about you on the back of it.

### Be realistic
An appearance on *Parkinson* will not be possible for everyone. Very few authors get mass-market advertising.

## What makes the ideal author from a publicist's point of view?

Tony Mulliken of Midas PR, a company that specialises in working in the publishing industry, assisted me with the following list for a recent seminar at the Society of Authors.

### Ten vulgar questions that a publicist would like to know the answer to:

(1) What do you look like? Would a photograph of you make journalists sit up and take notice?

(2) Who are you married to/have a relationship with at the moment? Who have you had a relationship with in the past that would be of interest to other people?

(3) Can you talk as well as write? Would you interview well?

(4) Who do you know – what useful contacts do you have?

(5) What's dramatic about you? What have you done in the past that could be turned into a useful story?

(6) What hobbies, or better still obsessions, do you have that we could make sound interesting?

(7) Who are your enemies? (Controversy can be wonderful forgetting publicity.) What kind of trouble have you run into in the past?

(8) Would you be willing to write articles for no money?

(9) Where do you live and what do your neighbours think of you? Are you willing to open your house up to the media?

(10) What is your relationship like with your family? Famous parents can be very useful as can 'black sheep relations' happy to bring a private dispute into the public domain.

## What is the most difficult type of author to promote from a publicist's point of view?

Someone who:

- sees their book as their final statement and won't add anything to it
- clams up when confronted by the media
- complains constantly about what has not been achieved rather than acknowledging the effort that has gone into the process; never says thank you for what has been achieved
- is immensely suspicious
- has no sense of humour
- doesn't respond to media interest immediately – if you delay they will be onto the next story.

## What are the media looking for?

There are a wide variety of different opportunities for media coverage. Bear in mind that for each type of coverage a different journalist is likely to be in charge, so there could be many different people on a particular outlet that you should keep in touch with.

- Review coverage – on the books page. Contact: the Reviews Editor.
- Feature coverage – through a specially commissioned article or interview. Contact: the Features Editor.
- Specific, regular spots in a paper – for example, 'Life in the Day of', in *The Sunday Times*, or regular programmes/columns such as ,'Desert Island Discs', or ,'What's in your fridge?'. Contact: each feature would have its own editor.
- News coverage. Contact: the News Editor.
- Diary coverage. Contact: find out the name of the piece and address it to the Editor.

They also need ideas, preferably those their competitors have not already thought of, which may be picked up by all of the above.

- Trade press. They will have all the above slots, for example the *Bookseller* has a diary/gossip column called 'Bent's Notes'.

## How to get the names of journalists

You may be familiar with many names from reading the papers. But these are often either staff or freelance writers who work under the direction of the 'section editor' for a particular area of the paper or programme. It is the section editor who directs what gets written about, and can commission new features on forthcoming matters of interest to the audience/readership.

So how do you get hold of their names? Firstly, you can build your own lists using a copy of a media yearbook. For example, the *Writers' and Artists' Yearbook* (A&C Black) includes addresses and contact numbers for national and local press and broadcast media. If you have time to do a personal mailshot, you could ring each specific medium and ask for the names of those you wish to contact (checking difficult spellings) and the address to which they would like material sent (often not the same as the general address of the paper in question). If you have less time you could just send your information to the relevant editor by job title at the address given.

Be rigorous in keeping records of those you have spoken to. Which is their day off, when is the best time to contact them? Journalists working on Sunday papers generally have Monday off, but their life becomes very frantic towards the end of the week as publication gets nearer.

Alternatively, there are several media agencies that specialise in maintaining lists of journalists. Probably the best known is PIMS UK (see Useful Addresses). You can order names by subject specialisation (for example, all journalists dealing with children's products) in a variety of formats (e-mail file, labels, etc.).

## Getting your timing right

Effective timing is crucial for achieving publicity. Why?

- Because it takes time to consider how best to secure coverage, to finalise and format your information attractively, for journalists to consider it, for proof copies of the book to be despatched and for the interviews to be arranged.
- Because you need to ensure that the publicity appears at the same time as the book is available for purchase, and this takes planning.

In the run up to publication, the publishing house's reps will (either personally or by telephone) try to persuade bookshops to take stock on the grounds that there will be demand. For this reason it is very important that any associated publicity should peak when the books are available in the shops. Bookshops have a very short period of time over which a book is deemed to be a success (and further stock ordered) or a failure (and stock sent back to the publisher). If the publicity is late, and the demand consequently delayed, the book may already be back with the publisher when the public start to ask for the title, and sales will probably never recover.

It follows that starting to think about publicity when the book comes out is no use at all. Publicity needs to be thought about a good six months before.

If an agent is negotiating your publishing contract, a figure to be spent on marketing and publicity is probably agreed then. If you are handling the negotiations yourself, this is something you will have to bring to your publisher's attention at that point. As Tony Mulliken of Midas PR said:

> My advice to authors wanting publicity is to rattle the cage, and do so early. The more fuss you make the more attention you will get.

How much to rattle the cage is a question of judgement. If you are constantly on the phone you may alienate, but do remind the publicist seriously and pro-actively about what you think is possible. Try to amalgamate your requests and contacts into reasonable chunks (rather than sending a memo every second day) and express them in a tone that combines passion with achievability.

## How to draw up a publicity plan

(1) Look at the book/product objectively and think about the options available.
(2) Decide what is achievable.
(3) Make a list of preferences.
(4) Follow them up (by e-mail, post or phone call, although not too often).

## What to send out to journalists

- A press release. This is the most basic document; for advice on how to write one, see Chapter 7.
- A copy of the book, or a proof or 'reading' copy, or the offer of a free copy on request.
- An associated freebie. This can work to attract a journalist's attention. Review copies of *Confessions of a Southern Lady* (Silver Moon Books) were sent out with a (very well packed!) miniature bottle of Southern Comfort. Be very wary of using humour however – ideas that seem funny initially can appear very different in the cold light of day when the post is received.
- A picture of the author with a caption on the back. Remember that images with lots of colour are more likely to be used than those with little, and that an interesting photo (with an interesting caption) is more likely to be used than a photograph showing a line-up of people holding drinks.

## Local press

Don't assume that only national media are worth pursuing. Local coverage can be very helpful as it offers:

- a direct vehicle to a particular market. If a book has a strong regional flavour, or the author strong local connections, try to get coverage in a local paper
- less of a hard-nosed approach than the nationals. This gives authors inexperienced with the publicity process the chance to practise dealing with the media
- extra opportunities for coverage. These exist where the author was born, went to school or university, where they live now and have lived previously, where their family came from and so on.

## What to do if a journalist won't take your calls or never takes up any of your ideas

Don't despair. Get to know the other people working on the desk. Even if it is not an extensive department there will almost certainly be a 'number two'. It follows that:

- they get fewer calls, so may be able to talk to you for longer
- if the ideas you suggest are sensible and interesting, they are a direct route to the main editor. Their voice behind an idea you suggest will have more weight than your own
- one day they will probably be the lead journalist themselves (either on the current slot or elsewhere), and if you have built up good relations you will have someone who will always take your calls.

## How to give an effective radio interview

An interview with a local radio station is often the starting point for an author's involvement in publicity. The interviewer's approach is unlikely to be aggressive; they will be more concerned with producing interesting listening than extracting a confession you don't want to give. Nevertheless, a few words of advice may be useful.

- Listen to the programme on which you are scheduled to appear for several days before your appointment. Concentrate on the interviewer's style; think about the questions you are likely to be asked and what kind of people are likely to be listening.
- Wear clothes that are comfortable, and avoid jangling bracelets (along the same lines, beware of filling up your glass with water whilst on the air – from the throaty gurgle, the listener will conclude you are imbibing much stronger stuff!).
- When the interview starts you will probably be nervous, so concentrate on listening to the questions asked rather than thinking about what you want to say. If an interview develops

as a conversation this will make you feel much more comfortable and produce more interesting listening.

- Do not prepare a statement to read out. This will sound wooden and unconvincing, and will tempt you to use words that are part of your written rather than your spoken vocabulary (and are therefore harder to understand). What is more, if the statement is part of the press release sent by a publishing house, the interviewer may use it to introduce you. Try to talk from memory, but with the three most important themes (headlines only!) that you must get over, whatever the questions asked, noted down in case your mind completely freezes.

> If the public have to make an effort to understand, they will not make the effort.
>
> Peter Hobday, *Managing the Message*,
> Allison and Busby

- The best preparation is to have thought around the subject matter of your book and of the possible questions. Can you get a friend to practice interviewing you so you get used to both the approach and the sound of your own voice? Likely questions include:
  - why did you write the book?
  - what is the book about?
  - who will read it?
  - how long did the writing/researching take you?
  - what are you planning to do next?
  - what advice do you have for other people who would like to write a book?
- If statistics are central to your argument, have one or two to hand (no more!) and try to express them in their simplest form (for example, 'half' rather than '50 per cent').
- Reread the book just before the interview. This is particularly important if you are now immersed in another project.

## Case Study 1: Getting publicity for an author in difficult circumstances

*Short Change* by Julia Notaro, Simon & Schuster

There were a number of problems in trying to achieve publicity for this author:

- first book from an unknown author based in Japan
- little time. The publicists (Midas PR) were only instructed to start work on the campaign in April for a May publication date, making it too late to set up trade press or magazine coverage
- author lives in rural Japan and was very difficult to contact. She works all day and so could only speak between 10.30pm–12.30 am British time or by e-mail, thus it always took at least 24 hours for a reply to questions. Her rural location (several hours from Tokyo) made it hard for journalists to visit her
- she did not arrive in Britain until six weeks after publication, which meant a loss of momentum after the first run of newspaper articles. The publicist set up a number of broadcast interviews to tie in with her visit, but lost several of them – including *This Morning* – because the story was deemed to be too old six weeks later.

The publicist, Vivienne Pattison, writes:

> The book had no strong features angles and it was very hard to create a story that would appeal to journalists. I therefore focused my campaign on the author's personal story which I sold as unusual. Later in the campaign, when a news story on sexism in the city broke, I was able to use the book and the author to give an insider's view on the problem.

In trying to achieve publicity, there is often one particular piece that marks a breakthrough, and really makes a difference. In this case it was interviews with the author which ran on the same day in the *Daily Mail* and the *Daily Express* which generated a lot of interest. This meant that when I rang broadcast contacts they were aware of the person I was offering them.

The promotion budget was nil, the only promotional item produced was a press release. This unpromising start yielded a huge number of interviews and coverage.

## Case Study 2: Overcoming media resistance

*Falling leaves* by Adeline Yen Mah, Penguin

It can be very difficult to achieve publicity for a title that is coming out in paperback, having been launched as a hardback. Many media outlets will not re-review a title that has already been published, however worthwhile.

The publicist's second difficulty was to convince journalists that this was an accessible story of human interest that would appeal to a wide variety of people; she feared that on first sight many would consider it too high-brow or political. As far as women's magazines were concerned, many of the more prominent titles felt that it wasn't UK-based enough to make it viable for them. Finally, as the story happened so long ago, she had to overcome a view amongst editors that this meant there was not enough of a hook for an interview with the author now.

> My key objective was to get them to read the press release – once they did that they were converted relatively quickly. I tried to impress upon the media that this should be considered as a global story of an unhappy and abused childhood, that could equally well apply to any child anywhere, not just in China. This definitely helped secure both the *Esther* programme (as part of a feature on children who are used as scapegoats) and the interview in *Frank* magazine.
>
> Lydia Drukarz

Promotional materials produced: press release and biographical information sheet.

# FALLING LEAVES
## An Unwanted Chinese Daughter
### by Adeline Yen Mah
Published on 2 April 1998 in paperback by Penguin Books at £6.99

'I was the ostracized outsider longing for acceptance; the ugly duckling hankering to return as the beautiful swan; the despised and unwanted Chinese daughter, obsessed with my quest to make my parents proud of me on some level. Surely if I tried hard enough to help in dire need, they would love me.'

Although she was born into an affluent and influential family in Shanghai during the 1930s, Adeline Yen Mah was spurned when her mother died giving birth to her, and her father remarried a beautiful yet cruel Eurasian. At the time, her Grand Aunt had formed the Shanghai Women's Bank and her father, having started his own firm at the age of nineteen, was known as the miracle boy with the power of turning iron into gold. Yet in the midst of this wealth, Adeline - the fifth child and youngest daughter - was discriminated against, neglected and emotionally and physically abused by the majority of her family throughout her childhood and teenage years. Even her siblings bullied and beat her. Only her Aunt Baba and her grandfather Ye Ye gave her love and encouragement.

**Falling Leaves** is a courageous and unfaltering account of how she survived that rejection and, despite being humiliated and belittled by her family in her adult life, went on to become a successful doctor in the United States. It is a poignant and enthralling story of a Chinese family, torn apart with hate and feuds, from the time of the foreign concessions in Shanghai to the rise of Communist China and the commercial boom of Hong Kong. Adeline struggled simply to survive and learned to rely only on her inner strength to help her achieve her goals: to come through the nightmare of her childhood and make something of herself one day.

The hardback of **Falling Leaves** was published by Michael Joseph earlier last year to great acclaim. Amy Tan has described it as: 'Riveting. A marvel of memory. Poignant proof of the human will to endure ...' and Adeline's story has been compared with Jung Chang's *'Wild Swans'*. Chang herself described it as: 'Charged with emotion ... A vivid portrait of the human capacity for meanness, malice - and love.' In addition, Adeline has already been approached by two American film producers interested in turning her story into a screenplay.

> Adeline Yen Mah will be available for interview and is also willing to write an article about her experiences. If you would be interested in talking to her, doing a feature/review on the book or even taking extracts from *Falling Leaves*, please contact Lydia Drukarz at Midas Public Relations on: 0171-584 7474.

---

## ADELINE YEN MAH
## Author of 'Falling Leaves: An Unwanted Chinese Daughter'

### BIOGRAPHICAL INFORMATION

Adeline Yen Mah was born into an affluent and influential family in Shanghai during the 1930's. At that time, her Grand Aunt had formed the Shanghai Women's Bank and her father, having started his own firm at the age of nineteen, was known as the miracle boy with the power of turning iron into gold. Yet in the midst of this wealth, Adeline - the fifth child and youngest daughter, suffered appalling emotional abuse.

Adeline's mother died in childbirth and her father remarried a beautiful but extremely cold and cruel Eurasian woman. At a time when everything western in treaty ports such as Shanghai was deemed superior to anything Chinese, the European-educated Niang (Chinese for 'stepmother') was the ultimate status symbol. Adeline's father was in her thrall. In their home in Shanghai, Niang treated the five stepchildren as second-class citizens. Adeline was especially singled out since she was thought to have brought bad luck to the family because her mother had died giving birth to her. Throughout her childhood and teenage years, she was discriminated against, neglected and emotionally and physically abused by the majority of her family. Her siblings bullied and beat her. Only her Aunt Baba and her grandfather Ye Ye gave her love and encouragement.

When in 1949, as the Red Army approached, the family moved to Hong Kong, Adeline was sent to boarding school, forbidden to receive visitors or post. While her father became one of Hong Kong's most successful businessmen, she was allowed home only three times. She dreamed of freedom and independence.

Against a backdrop of changing political times and the collision of East and West, Adeline struggled simply to survive and relied on her inner strength to help her achieve her goals: to come through the nightmare of her childhood and make something of herself one day. She studied extremely hard at school and, although originally she had yearned to become a writer, again she bowed to her father's wishes and went on to study medicine at Oxford, trying always to gain his approval. Despite the fact that her family continued to humiliate and belittle her throughout her adult life, she moved to America and succeeded in becoming an anaesthetist and, later, director of a prosperous medical practice in California. She married a kind and understanding Chinese-American called Bob and had two children.

Later on in her life, she gave up her directorship of the practice to concentrate full-time on writing an account of her turbulent and harrowing childhood. **Falling Leaves** is that account. It is a courageous and unfaltering account of how she survived the rejection and cruelty, and is told with dignity, yet she still shows no bitterness towards those who mistreated her.

She currently divides her time between London and the United States.

## *Why did this strategy work?*
Lydia Drukarz, for Midas Public Relations comments:

I feel that the review coverage, together with the wide range of television coverage, really helped establish *Falling*

*Leaves* as a bestseller, and brought it to the attention of a real cross-section of the book public.

The book appeals on many levels – firstly as a general human interest story, on the abused childhood angle, it reaches out to those who have been through something similar, and finally to those readers who appreciate a well-written and gripping story.

In addition to the above, the fact that the publicity campaign was spread out over a period of many months helped to keep the sales buoyant. Adeline first came over to the UK for three weeks. She then came back in August to speak at the Edinburgh Book Festival and to do publicity in Ireland. Whilst in the UK in August, she recorded the *Bookworm* programme, which was finally aired in October. This gave us several opportunities to remind the public that the book was still out there, and kept it in their minds.

## Case Study 3: Getting publicity for a project which involves lots of different collaborators at the same time

*Girls' Night In*, Harper Collins 2000, is a collection of 31 short stories by 31 female authors, published to raise funds for the charity War Child.

Melody Odusanya, Senior Account Manager at Colman Getty, who handled publicity for the project, comments as follows:

> Liaising with so many authors at the same time was complicated and we found group e-mail contact and the delegation of specific tasks (for example, coordinating the event schedule, organising the launch party, managing the overall media campaign, targeting authors regionally) worked well. Another problem we faced was that some of the individual authors had new books to promote at around the same time and we did not wish to confuse the press. We also had to work hard to pitch some of the slightly lesser known authors and ensure the charity War Child got coverage too.

The press release is shown below. This prompted lots of author interviews and features, especially in the regional press, and the book has sold very well – it has already been reprinted several times.

---

*Treat yourself to a Girls' Night In, and help raise money for War Child...*

# GIRLS' NIGHT IN

## A collection of short stories by some of today's most talented young writers

*To be published as a paperback original on 3<sup>rd</sup> July 2000, price £5.99, in aid of War Child*

One evening, three novelist friends met up for drinks. During their chitchat, they started a discussion about the host of young women whose fiction currently tops the book charts. The three novelists decided to try and bring all that talent together in one book for one terrific cause close to their hearts – **War Child**, the charity that provides support and assistance to children caught up in the horrors of war.

The brainchild of writing friends Jessica Adams, Chris Manby and Fiona Walker, **Girls' Night In** is a must-have collection of original short stories from the very best of contemporary women novelists from the UK, Ireland, USA and Australia.

**All the authors donated their stories. They are:**

Jessica Adams, Yasmin Boland, Claire Calman, Jenny Colgan, Rosalyn Chissick, Tiffanie Darke, Stella Duffy, Wendy Holden, Sarah Ingham, Amy Jenkins, Lisa Jewell, Cathy Kelly, Marian Keyes, Helen Lederer, Alecia McKenzie, Pauline McLynn, Chris Manby, Anna Maxted, Karen Moline, Clare Naylor, Freya North, Sheila O'Flanagan, Jane Owen, Adele Parks, Victoria Routledge, Polly Samson, Patricia Scanlan, Helen Simpson, Fiona Walker, Daisy Waugh and Isabel Wolff.

**At least one pound for every copy of *Girls' Night In* sold will go to War Child.**

Set up in 1993 in response to the plight of children in former Yugoslavia, **War Child** was founded upon a fundamental goal: to advance the cause of peace through investing in the lives of children caught up in the horrors of war.

Initially raising money through entertainment events and public appeals, the charity set out to bring immediate material help to children of all ages and ethnic backgrounds.

Since it's inception, **War Child** has alleviated the suffering of tens of thousands of children throughout the world. Providing food, clothing and medical equipment, **War Child** directs aid where it's needed most.

As the charity grew it was able to undertake larger projects and now provides food, communications, educational and social welfare programmes in many countries. Critically, it does not disappear when the guns have stopped shooting and the fires have died down. **War Child** is also instrumental in healing the psychological damage caused to children by their experiences of war.

**War Child** has received tremendous support from a great many well-known figures, including **Stella McCartney**, **Kate Moss**, **Neil Morrissey**, **David Bowie**, **Hugo Speer**, **Tom Stoppard** and **Johnny Depp**.

"War Child is a cool, funky outfit run by very hands-on people. And you can see the benefit of efforts almost immediately."
**Neil Morrissey**

"*Girl's Night In* is such a brilliant idea and it's been great watching it come together. War Child has tremendous admiration for all those involved. It is wonderful that a book that will bring so much pleasure to people around the world will also add a little hope to children whose lives have been devastated by conflict."
**Lynne Kuschel MBE, War Child**

**The money raised through the publication of *Girls' Night In* – at least £1 for every copy sold - will fund two essential projects:**

- The **Safe Play Areas Programme** runs throughout the **Balkans** on land cleared of mines, unexploded bombs and rubble. The aim is simple - **War Child** builds playgrounds where children of all ethnic backgrounds can play without fear, encouraging them to make friends across ethnic divides and build bridges for the future.

- In **Rwanda**, girls rarely have the opportunity to be educated into their teens - in fact as few as 8% complete primary school. In partnership with *Girls' Night In*, **War Child** will fund essential improvements to a **School of Excellence for Girls** in **Kigali**, ensuring that a greater number of young Rwandan women are given the opportunities taken for granted throughout the West.

**Fiona Walker, author and co-editor of *Girls' Night In*, comments:**

"We think that there are two things every child should be free to do – play and read. And as well as distributing vital food and medical supplies, War Child has another essential goal – to put the child back into the child. This book is unashamedly fun, joyful and escapist. In the Balkans, children will swing, slide, whirl around and roly-poly without fear of land mines. And in Rwanda, more girls will be educated not only to broaden their chances, but to open up a written world hitherto denied to them. We hope that, thanks to this book, many kids will laugh, shriek and escape whenever they please."

From disastrous dates to office politics, fading careers, internet trysts, seedy stalkers and love triangles on trains, *Girls' Night In* features something that every girl in the land will relate to – a powerful, feminine combination of 'girlie' issues and humour.

If you only read one book this summer, it has to be *Girls' Night In*.

-ends-

**Notes to Editors**

- **Please reference: *Girls' Night In* will be published on 3rd July 2000 by Harper Collins at £5.99. At least £1.00 from every book sold will be donated to War Child.**

- Most of the authors who have contributed to the book are available for interview. Please contact Sally, Caitlin or Melody at Colman Getty PR.

- Extract rights for *Girls' Night In* are available. To discuss extracts (with proceeds going to War Child), please contact Tara Wynne at Curtis Brown on 020 7396 6600 or email tara@curtisbrown.co.uk

- A charity launch party for *Girls' Night In* will take place at The October Gallery, Holborn on Thursday 29th June 2000. For further details please contact Melody at Colman Getty PR

- By buying this book you have already given one pound to **War Child**. If you would like to invest more please send donations to: War Child, PO Box 20231, London NW5 3DG.

- For further information on **War Child** please contact Lynne Kuschel or James Topham on 020 7916 9276 or visit the website at www.warchild.org.uk

- For further information about HarperCollins titles visit the website at www.fireandwater.com

**All media enquiries should be directed to:**

**Melody Odusanya, Sally Randall or Caitlin Raynor at
Colman Getty PR on 020 7439 1783
E-mail: melody@colmangettypr.co.uk
or sally@colmangettypr.co.uk or caitlin@colmangettypr.co.uk**

## Case study 4: Using information that is interesting to the media but has nothing to do with the subject matter of the book

I was pregnant with my second child whilst writing my first book, *How to Market Books*[1]. Delivery date of both child and book loomed and it was a race to see which would come first. In the end I finished the book four days before my daughter was born.

My publishers sent out a press release explaining the benefits of the book and this was picked up by the local paper who came round to do an interview on me as a local author. It was the photographer's idea to take a picture of book and baby together, and my son snuck into the shot too. This had nothing to do with the subject matter of the book at all but prompted useful coverage in the trade press as well.

### Mum's new baby's a book!

YOUNG mum Mrs. Alison Baverstock has opened a new chapter in her life, by bringing out her first book.

Alison, who lives in Mathews Road, Camberley, spent a year preparing and writing her book "How to Market Books".

She drew on her experience in publishing, followed by five years as a freelance publicity agent.

Now running her own marketing consultancy with a friend, Alison felt that she has took the time and the experience to write such a book.

"There is no other book on the market that gives information on such a topic.

"For that reason I found it fairly easy to find a publisher — in fact it was only the second one I approached.

"I set myself a deadline to get it finished before my baby Harriet was born, but in the end it came dangerously close to not getting done."

Baby and book came just four days apart.

The aim of the book is to give practical advice to publishers on increasing sales.

Alison hopes to write a novel as her next project.

"It has always been an ambition of mine," she said.

"How to Market Books," is published by Kogan Page, priced £12.95.

Alison with son Alasdair baby Harriet and her book

[1] *How to Market Books*, Alison Baverstock, Kogan Page, 3rd edition 1999, £17.99

# 9. How to Organise a Launch Event

Authors often associate the publication of a book with a launch party. Although 20 years ago this was not uncommon, today launch parties are relatively rare. Financial realities have hit home and publishers have to be sure that a real benefit will accrue from the holding of a celebratory event on publication. Such benefits could include:

- **press coverage**. The right chemistry at a party (a mix of journalists and interesting people) can produce a complimentary feature in the media. This could include news coverage, mentions in gossip and diary columns, a feature in the trade press which is read by booksellers, and so on
- an effective gathering can promote **word of mouth recommendations** about a book and encourage people to read the book in question, particularly if those invited are inclined to talk about what they have been to or read
- **keeping the author and their agent happy**. This can bring loyalty to the house and prolong the future relationship.

Whilst it doesn't follow that the lack of an offer of a party for your forthcoming book means no interest, you may decide to either help the publishers organise something (with them hopefully bearing the costs) or to organise something yourself. To follow are a few guidelines on how to run a successful event.

## What kind of event?

The most common form of book launch is a pre-dinner drinks party, say from 6.30–8.00 pm. Light snacks and drinks are provided, on the assumption that people will arrive around 6.45–7.00 pm and will be going on to eat somewhere else.

A drinks party has the benefit of being fairly simple to organise. But as this is the most frequently held kind of event, you may decide that something different is more appropriate. For example, you could consider the following:

### Breakfast

As breakfast is so often a hurried meal, or missed altogether, the chance to sit down and enjoy one in interesting company can be very appealing.

For example, a local religious bookshop of mine has started running regular breakfasts for the clergy on Friday mornings, a day that many clergy apparently have off. This offers them the chance to meet each other and hear about forthcoming products and offers. They find they get a very good take-up and that a lot of business results.

### A talk followed by lunch

To launch the Church of England's new liturgy, Common Worship, in November 2000, the designers Omnific staged an exhibition in the St Bride Printing Library, offered personal tours around it, followed by a finger buffet lunch (jointly hosted by Church House Publishing) afterwards.

### A demonstration connected with the subject of your book followed by refreshments

When promoting a book on the physicist Faraday, I once organised a demonstration of his most famous experiments in the lecture theatre where he first showed them to the world.

### A stunt linked to your book

Catherine Charley embarked on a new series of factual books for Puffin – Extreme Expeditions. 'I arrived at Waterstones in the centre of Belfast on a sledge pulled by a team of six huskies! This all linked into the theme of one of the books, The Big Freeze, which is about expeditions in the Arctic and Antarctic. TV, radio and newspapers all turned up and there was some great publicity as a result.'

---

### An event that has nothing to do with the book but is appealing to the market

Education Direct organised a presentation on their new database, 'Spirit', followed by a trip on the London Eye for all those who attended. This got a very good response.

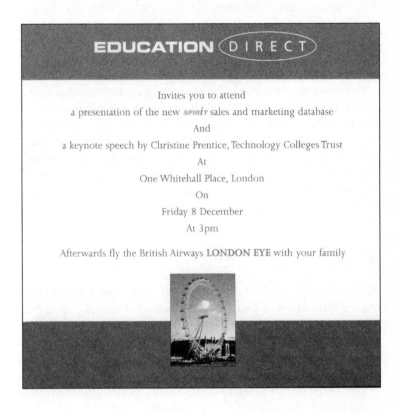

Whatever the format you eventually decide on, it's vital to consider the following:

- **what do you want out of it?** Will the event you are planning permit this? For example, if it is crucial for you as the author to have an intimate chat with a particular journalist, then a party may not be the best way to achieve this. Would going out to lunch be more successful?

- **how much time do the key people you want to be there have at their disposal?** Unless your event is mind-blowingly arresting, it's most likely pointless to organise an all-day event if you are trying to get the attention of busy press people who have only half an hour at most to spare
- **is there a synergy between function and format?** Breakfast is delicious but messy. Does it provide enough time and space for writing/interviewing if this is integral to what you want to achieve?
- **do you feel comfortable with what is suggested?** A hapless press event is probably more interesting to the media than one that runs smoothly, so do ensure that you can carry off whatever is suggested. For example, if you are a keen hiker, then climbing a mountain and handing a copy of your book on rural Wales to the press at the bottom may be very successful. If, however, despite immense knowledge of your subject, age these days prevents you from straying far from your car, you may end up looking ridiculous.

## Where to hold your event?

There are probably lots of venues that have experience of hosting the kind of event you have in mind. Alternatively, rack your brain for some new inspiration! For example:

- many local bookshops have room to stage an event. This has the advantage of fitting in with their own PR plans (i.e. they may help fund the event), and books, and the mechanisms for selling them, will be there already
- a local historic house or building (or its garden, depending on the time of year)
- a friend with a large house able to accommodate the event
- a local hotel (again, the manager may deem this good for PR and not charge you)
- a 'grunge' event. A completely unlikely location might attract media attention – perhaps a car park or a railway station waiting room (permission will be needed).

• Wherever you decide on, find out about the practical details:

– is access easy? If not, forget it
– is the venue interesting? Has it been overused by similar events or is it innovative?
– what about parking?
– do they have a license to serve drink (i.e. it is there already) or do you have to bring your own?
– are there enough loos for the assembled company?
– what about coats and umbrellas – where will they be put?
– what about glasses, cutlery and plates?
– are there chairs for those who can't stand up?

## When to hold your event?

Timing is very important. You need to consider time of year, time of week, time of day.

• Avoid Friday and Saturday evenings – most people have their own plans.
• Monday is a bad day if you want the Sunday press to attend; it is usually their journalists' day off.
• Summer holidays – often known as the silly season, but a great time for attracting attention to an appropriate story.
• Watch out for public holidays, paying particular attention to those you don't celebrate yourself – for example, Halloween (31 October), Burns Night (25 January). Either avoid them or tie your event in with the public occasion.
• Avoid regular and scheduled mass media interest events. For example, American Presidential elections are always on the first Tuesday of November, every four years; the inauguration is two months later.
• Do you want people to nip in after work or make an evening of it? If the latter, the chances are they will stay longer and drink more!

## Who to invite?

- Representatives of the media (broadcast and print) likely to be interested. Find out the names of the relevant editors and ask them, and the features writers who write for them. Be sure to include the local media.
- Celebrities who will add a buzz to the event.
- Other high profile people who have a connection with the subject matter of the book.
- Local booksellers.
- Friends and relations (keep this list moderate – whilst you don't wish it to look like a family reunion, a group of loyal retainers adds atmosphere to an event for those just arriving). Do encourage your contacts to talk to people other than those they know already.
- Those involved with the production of the book – freelance editors, proofreaders, illustrators, and so on. Often forgotten and can be very resentful.

## How far ahead to invite?

Send your invitations too far ahead and they risk getting lost, too close and those you invite may already be committed. About six weeks prior to the event is good.

## What to send with the invitation

The invitation (preferably printed so it looks professional and easy to read) should include all the relevant details:

- who is doing the inviting? (Company, individual or both, for example: the Managing Director and staff of. . . )
- if there is a keynote speaker already in place you may want to mention them on the invitation
- title and publisher of what is being launched
- place
- date

- time
- dress (casual/informal/formal/black tie)
- who should recipients reply to and how (telephone, fax, e-mail, etc.)
- is there any information you need prior to the event (for example, for security considerations do you need car registration numbers, etc.)?

Accompanying it should be a press release (see Chapter 7) giving further details of the project. This could include interesting information about the author, the book and the event/party being organised, where further information can be gained from and how to get a review copy of the book.

## Preparations before the event

- Confirm all arrangements *in writing* with the venue; never rely on conversations to confirm the details. Find out who will actually be running your event on the day: often this is not the person who took the booking from you.
- Find out what furniture is available to you. Are there enough tables on which to mount a display and are table coverings available? If not bring some (freshly ironed!) sheets.
- Organise sustenance. In general, more white wine than red will be drunk, and do ensure there are plenty of soft drinks – you will probably need more of these than you think.
  For a cocktail party offer food that can be eaten with the minimum of mess; avoid things that spurt butter or drip. Ask those handing food round to be methodical about approaching everyone. It can be frustrating to see food drifting past and not be offered any. They don't need to interrupt a conversation to offer food – the arrival of a tray and the engagement of eye contact can be enough to provide the opportunity. Some hosts lay out a table of food and encourage guests to help themselves; this can disrupt conversations and gives the added difficulty that the greediest will eat everything!
  If you are instructing caterers, you will need to confirm the

numbers likely to attend a week before, and will be charged per head on this figure, even if fewer than planned attend.

- Ensure there is someone on the door directing where coats should be put and armed with a complete list of names of everyone attending. Tick the names off as people arrive. Alternatively, ask people to sign a visitors book so you capture their names and addresses for future use (mailing them information on your next book).
- Do you plan to have name badges so all present can see the names of those they talk to? Make the badges large enough to allow space for a size of text that is readable.
- Ask the publisher *in writing* for stock of the book well before the launch. This sounds obvious, but if you don't ask for them, they may get overlooked. Double check that the stock is on its way two weeks before.

Bear in mind that many of those attending will see it as their right to walk away with a free copy of the book. Remember that the perceived value of a give-away is vastly out of proportion with the actual cost to the publisher – production costs may be no more than 10 per cent of the finished cost of the item. But if this is a problem (for example, if you have to pay for the books taken away, or the publisher does not wish them to be handed out and so erode the basic market), have someone guard them!

## A speaker

Events to promote a book need a focus; someone needs to stand and say why everyone is gathered and draw attention to key things about the project in question. Who should do the talk? I feel it's better for the author not to do it – it's difficult to deliver a panegyric yourself. But do reply.

Ask someone who others there are interested in meeting. They may do it for you, even if extremely busy, because:

- they like to be helpful
- the publicity will do them good

- they are keen to be associated with the project/cause you are promoting.

## What those present should take away from such an event

Have a **press pack** available to the media. This is usually a folder including:

- a copy of the book
- a press release
- an author photograph (with a caption saying who it is and the name of the book on the back)
- contact details
- relevant information on other titles, for example, how well did the author's last title sell?
- the promotional plans for the title. This gives the journalist a sense of scale, i.e. how important this author is.

Offer everyone else the chance to buy the book. Either ask a local bookseller to come along and offer copies for sale, or order stock and get a friend to sell them for you. Ensure they have a stock of change (most book prices end in 99p) and that cheques get signed!

If the party is being held prior to the publication date, you will need to consult the publisher on whether sales can be made. You may be asked to refer sales to bookshops after publication instead.

## Photographs

Will the publisher provide for the services of a freelance photographer to take pictures at the event? If not, is it worth arranging one yourself – or just equipping a friend with a camera?

Don't rely on photographers to know who/what you wish to be photographed. Brief them beforehand on what you want (relatively straightforward if they will recognise who they are meant to be photographing). Alternatively, send a friend or colleague who knows what you are looking for and get them to accompany the photographer around the room.

On the grounds that 'he who pays the piper calls the tune' ask that the photographer dresses appropriately. At a very smart event a photographer wearing jeans and a T-shirt will stand out like a sore thumb.

## Follow up after a launch event

Send captioned photos to the media who did not attend but seemed interested. Attach an accompanying press release saying how successful it was. Do you have any anecdotal feedback worth passing on? Can you provide some yourself? For example: 'It seems prawn lovers adore Catherine Jones's books. And they descended en masse on a book launch in Waterstones on Tuesday last. Within 5 minutes of arrival there were absolutely none left! The reason for this difficult decision. . . ' . Or 'Beaujolais Nouveau hits Kingston. The Wilson Hall was packed last Friday as wine lovers eager to sample the new vintage stampeded into the first place in Surrey to have any. As you can see from the attached picture, daringly taken by our intrepid photographer. . . '.

## Why your publisher should bear the costs of a launch you have organised yourself

- You have done all the organisation for them; thus they save staff time and effort.
- Your organisation will cost a fraction of what it would have cost to get professional caterers to do it for them.
- It's very good PR for their publishing house.
- It's an excellent chance for them to display other titles from their range (you could offer their catalogues for display).
- If you invite representatives of the local book trade, it can promote relations with their key customers.

# 10. How to Be the Perfect Speaker

It may interest you to know that once you have written a book, there will be many organisations that would like to hear you speak. They may be keen on the particular subject matter of your book, or perhaps a completely different topic, but the fact that you have written something of book length, and had it published, marks you out as someone worth listening to. This chapter provides advice on how to make the most of the opportunity.

## Where to speak?

There are standard organisations that meet at regular intervals in most centres of population: civic societies, Round Table, language clubs, etc; your local council should be able to provide some information to get you started. Ours offers a printed list (copy available free on request) of all organisations that relate to young people, and a council-run website for the area as a whole.

It is worth bearing in mind that the vitality of each organisation is a direct function of how lively those running it are, and this will obviously vary from region to region. You cannot assume that because the branch of a specific organisation in your own town is completely moribund, that others will be too.

In addition to looking at official lists of organisations, it is also worth finding out about the following.

• Which organisations your friends and colleagues belong to, and which offer the kind of programme that is most naturally suited to you. With which organisations could friends put in a good word for you?

- Are there any particularly active organisations in your area
- Read the correspondence columns and look at the advertisements for forthcoming events in the local paper to pick up ideas.
- Are there any organisations linked to your local bookshop? Several shops now organise literary breakfasts and lunches in local venues in addition to the more familiar evening readings.
- Look at the notice boards in your local library and ask about related associations at the information desk. Leaflets on local societies are often available here, too.
- Find out about relevant festivals both in your area and further afield. Literary festivals are the obvious starting point, but general town festivals and flower festivals often have accompanying programmes of talks from visiting speakers.
- What about educational institutions in the neighbourhood? Are there any well-known schools, a university, adult education college or further education college? Offer to speak at one such institution, and make a good job of it, and you may find your name passed on to others.

For each of the above, you need to know:

- when they meet
- where they meet
- the length of the meetings
- at what stage in the proceedings the talk takes place, for example over breakfast or after dinner
- how many people are likely to attend
- the kind of people – and their particular interests – that generally come along
- name, address and contact number(s) of the person who books speakers (often called the Programme Secretary).

Bear in mind that there is often a long time period between sending information and being approached – one author told me recently of an 18-year wait!

## What to send out to advertise your services

- A letter to the person who books speakers, introducing yourself and providing details of how to contact you.
- An information sheet on your book (perhaps a copy of the advance notice – see Chapter 4 – or a sheet produced by your publisher). Even if your talk is unrelated to your book, something proving that the book exists is a good idea. Remember that your offer will most likely be discussed at a committee meeting so the more interesting/impressive the information you send on yourself, the more likely you are to be approached for a booking.
- A list of options of what you could talk about (see page 117-18).
- Feedback from those who have heard you speak before. This is perhaps best set out as a list of quotations, all shown in inverted commas with the names and organisations they represent listed. Don't just put initials – it then sounds as though they are not genuine comments. As to where to get such testimonials, remember that it is standard practice for Programme Secretaries to write after the event to thank you, and it is perfectly permissible to quote from these letters.

## What you could offer

Before you contact such organisations to offer your services, it is a good idea to draw up a short menu of options with which to tempt them. I would recommend including several items on the list so that if the most obvious choice does not appeal, another on your list may be considered. Keep the wording short and snappy – if they do decide to use you it will probably form the basis of the programme entry.

## Marketing Your Book:
## An Author's Guide

Alison Baverstock

Authors will benefit hugely from this practical book by seeing how effective they can be at helping to promote their own books. Alison Baverstock encourages authors to work with publishers but also explains how to 'go it alone' for authors who plan to self publish.

The book covers:
• how marketing works
• what opportunities there are
• how authors can help
• how to get noticed
• how to get local publicity, organise a launch event and keep the momentum going after publication.

The book also provides authors with a real insight into the publishing process and contains illuminating interviews with everyone concerned: editors, marketing people and, most importantly, authors.

**KEY SELLING POINTS**

• a must for all authors and would-be authors

• gives useful, practical advice

• empowers and motivates authors

### series: **Writing Handbooks**

| SUBJECT | EDITION | BINDING | FORMAT (mm) | EXTENT | ILLUSTRATIONS |
|---|---|---|---|---|---|
| Writing/ marketing | 1st | pb | 216x135 | 160pp | – |

## Author(s)

Alison Baverstock has worked in publishing as a marketing manager and publicity controller and now works freelance as a marketing and management consultant. She lectures on publishing courses at City University, London and regularly gives talks on the industry. She is also the author of Kogan Page's *How to Market Books* – now in its third edition.

| PRICE |
|---|
| £9.99 |

| ISBN |
|---|
| 0 7136 5965 3 |

| PUBLICATION DATE |
|---|
| AUG 2001 |

ISBN 0-7136-5965-3

| | MARKET RESTRICTIONS | |
|---|---|---|
| AUTHOR LOCATION | US PUBLISHER | OTHER? |
| KINGSTON-UPON-THAMES | – | – |

A & C Black (Publishers) Limited, PO Box 19, St Neots, Cambs PE19 8SF tel: 01480 212666 fax: 01480 405014 email:sales@acblack.com
Editorial, publicity and rights: 37 Soho Square, London W1D 3QZ tel: 020 7758 0200 fax: 020 7758 0222 email:enquiries@acblack.com

**Send a copy of the advance notice to prove the book exists**

## Alison Baverstock

I could talk about:

**How to get a book published**

If you feel you 'have a book in you', how should you go about getting it out? Which are the most sensible publishing houses to approach, and do you need an agent before you start? How likely are you to get accepted straightaway and how do you keep your morale going – and keep writing – when you receive rejection letters? What does it feel like to see your name in print? I can offer first-hand, practical advice, having now had six books published.

**How books are made**

What happens in the making of a book, from the moment the manuscript is delivered to the appearance of final copies? How long does the whole process take and who makes all the main decisions? Publishers refer to books which they turned down but a rival house had a great success with as 'the ones that got away'. So why was Harry Potter's true merit lost on so many houses? A fascinating insight into the world of publishing from someone who has worked in the industry for over 20 years.

Alison Baverstock

**How to set up a reading circle**

Reading circles (or literary groups as they are sometimes called) are the hottest trend in reading Britain – it was recently estimated that there are now over 30,000, and someone has just written a book on this (essentially Anglo-Saxon) phenomenon. So if you have longed to join a book circle, but not yet found one to join, why not set up your own?

I have now set up six reading circles, all of which are still running. What is the genesis of a good reading group? Supper or wine? Male, female or mixed company? Who should choose the books and how often should you meet?

All the above talks are adaptable for groups of children, with the addition of props and dressing up clothes.

## What you should get out of it

Some organisations will pay a fee; others offer travelling expenses; some may offer both. If the event includes a meal of some kind, you should not be expected to pay for yours.

What level of fee to suggest is difficult. If you are speaking to a large audience from a multi-national company, they will most likely be comfortable paying a vastly higher fee than a local primary school with absolutely no budget for such events. As a guideline, a useful figure to quote is the Society of Authors' recommended rate of £150 for half a day and £200 for a full day, and this is in line with levels of expenditure approved by regional arts boards.

Travelling expenses will normally be added to this – the usual practice is to charge for a second class return rail fare, along with additional taxis and buses – but most organisations will require you to keep the receipts for reimbursement. Alternatively, you may be able to use your car at a certain amount per mile. If you have to stay overnight then accommodation may be offered at a committee member's house rather than the society having to incur a hotel bill. If you are offered such hospitality, do remember to write and thank your host – a failure to do so can be remembered long after your scintillating performance.

More useful to you still is the opportunity to sell copies of your book. This can be done at the end of the event, and it may help to encourage people to part with their money there and then if you offer a special discount to those present. Your publisher may be willing to provide leaflets to hand out/place on seats and a showcard to advertise the book and its price.

A good alternative option is to have your book included in the price of the seat, so each member of the audience gets a copy of the book to have signed and go away with. You may have to give the organisers a substantial discount on the book's selling price to encourage this, but this is often popular with organisers as it represents very good value to the audience. Alternatively, offer ticket prices which include a discount on the book, as the following example shows.

Of a more practical nature, if you are going to take stock of your book with you to sell, and wish to display it, you need to put someone in charge of selling/looking after it. You don't want to be put in the difficult position of stock going missing and as a result the event costing you money. Take along a receipt pad so that you can offer those who buy proof of purchase – useful if the book is likely to be claimed as a business expense.

Silver Moon Women's Bookshop

invites you to an evening with

SANDI TOKSVIG

talking about her new novel

Flying Under Bridges

Wednesday 2nd May 2001 at 7pm
The Royal Geographical Society
1 Kensington Gore, London SW7

Tickets £5.00 (£2.00 from ticket price will
be redeemable from the price of books
purchased on the night)

Published by Little, Brown

At an evening introduced by
Jenni Murray

Tickets available in advance from
Silver Moon Women's Bookshop
64-68 Charing Cross Road
London WC2H 0BT

Tel: 020 7836 7906

smwb@silvermoonbookshop.co.uk
www.silvermoonbookshop.co.uk

## Things to do before the day

### Find out about the group you are talking to

What is the average age of members? What kind of talks have gone down particularly well/bombed in the past? How many questions are there likely to be?

Ask the person who books you to confirm all the details in writing beforehand. If they do not, write to them and confirm your understanding of what has been agreed. Ring a week beforehand to double-check. Not all voluntarily run societies are as efficient as you might hope.

Is any publicity planned? Will a photographer from the local press be present? Navigating the difficult line between being a pushy person and a useful source of ideas is made easier for the organisers if they appreciate the benefits they will reap if an event goes well (better known society with more members, more widely attended meetings in future, other good speakers willing to come and talk).

### Think about the format of your talk

How long should you talk for? Remember to allow plenty of time for questions, and if you think these are going to be slow coming, suggest a couple to your contact in the organisation that they could perhaps ask themselves to get things moving.

Ask who is going to introduce you and if they need any more information about you in order to do an effective job. Ask them to phone you if they would like to talk to you in further detail.

Remember that different groups have very different dynamics and you will be catapulted into this, and expected to be flexible. For example, I gave a talk to a Working Parents Association recently. The evening began (rather surprisingly) with everyone introducing themselves on the basis of their name, their job and their childcare arrangements. I duly followed suit. I found that as I talked the audience liked to comment on every point I made, so each theme was discussed by those present (about 20) before moving onto the next one. Once I got used to this it was a pleasant way to proceed. I was able to get a feel for their sympathies and respond to them as I talked, and also did not have to do all the talking – although monitoring how far we should stray from the subject also fell to me.

## What to take with you

**Very brief notes or headings on which you can expand**
Never, ever, read a speech. As Michael Barratt, host of *Nationwide* and a hugely experienced television and radio presenter, put it:

> I still recommend those who are going to be addressing audiences regularly to try to develop the art of speaking ad lib. It's hard work. It means mentally rehearsing a logically progressive theme (not learning the actual words) over and over again until you have it clear-cut in the mind.
>
> The best way to do this, in my experience, is to write down five or six one-word 'headlines' of the argument you want to pursue. See whether they make a sensible progression, building to a rational conclusion. Then commit them to memory. You may also like to write them down on a small card which can easily be referred to if memory fails when you're standing there and the mind goes completely blank.
>
> Developing this skill will have two main effects. It will help you to get across your message much more effectively by using conversational rather than written English. And it will gradually develop your confidence in changing tack when that vital 'listening' process tells you it's necessary to do so.
>
> *Making the Most of the Media*, Kogan Page, 1996

**Props**
Samples of what you are talking about. The editor who deals with arts and crafts titles for one publisher routinely takes along pots to be handed round whilst she is talking. This makes points instantly comprehensible and is a lovely way of drawing the audience in.

**Local colour**
Try to make what you say sound as though it is written for the audience you address; make it personal. I find it is a good idea to start with a reference to something topical or local. If you get the chance, try to pick up a copy of the local paper the same day and flick through to find out what are current concerns/ interesting topics in the area, or talk briefly to your host.

**A sense of occasion**
Think carefully about what to wear. There will be many attending but only one speaker, so don't imagine that nobody in the audience will notice what you are wearing. On the contrary, they will be considering what you are wearing, whether or not they are conscious of it, for the duration of your talk. Try to match your outfit to the group in hand. For a formal evening event you need to know what the dress code is; for an afternoon discussion with an informal audience a more relaxed approach will be necessary. If, for political or social reasons, you decide to break a dress code (for example, Gordon Brown wearing a lounge suit rather than the more usual white tie to the annual Mansion House dinner) it should be a deliberate decision rather than the result of failing to do your homework.

## And afterwards. . .

A note of thanks for an effective evening is always appreciated. Thank your host for everything organised and say they are free to pass on your name to colleagues doing a similar job for other organisations. And prepare for the phone to ring. . .

# 11. Keeping the Momentum Going After Publication

For the writer preparing a book, the delivery date dominates for months ahead. And during the final weeks before delivery it is all consuming; one can think of little else. But once the manuscript has been handed over, it is the publication date that takes over as the key date.

## What happens on publication?

Publishers announce a title's publication date 6–9 months in advance. This is the date on which the selling of stock may begin (although it is sometimes ignored to secure a competitive advantage). About three weeks before publication is the 'release date', when titles are sent out to bookshops in preparation for publication.

At about this time books are also sent out to review editors for them to commission reviews from their regular writers. When the reviews actually appear may vary – reviews for mass-market fiction may appear within a couple of weeks of publication. For academic titles, which are reviewed in irregularly published journals, the process may take months.

For the fortunate, publication may be accompanied by requests for interviews, appearances in the broadcast media and local events, perhaps a book signing in a local store or an interview with the local paper.

## What do you do after publication?

With luck, you will already have embarked on your next writing job – indeed, it can be quite difficult at publication to focus on what is by now your previous book (so be sure to re-read it before any interviews take place).

## What is your long term aim?

Particularly if this is your first book, this is a good time to think about your motivation. Adapting the French proverb about food, do you write to live or live to write? Or given the economics of writing, do you do neither; does some other activity subsidise your writing? How serious are you about your writing? Consider the following questions.

- How do you describe yourself on forms you have to fill in; at parties?
- What do your family describe you as? Is it the same term you would use?
- Are you an author or a writer? I tend to think of authors as writing fiction and writers as those who turn their hand to most things, for example journalism.
- What professional associations or writers' groups do you belong to?

## Authors in the wider world

For me, having a book published was a personal pinnacle. It was something I had wanted to achieve for a very long time, and finally seeing my name in print was immensely satisfying. I cried. Not everyone sees it as quite so important.

- Car insurers are suspicious, often asking for special terms from writers.
- Having had various jobs in the book trade, I have experimented with various job titles on my name badge at the

London Book Fair. The one that aroused least eye contact and most averted gazes was 'author'.

- If you *are* successful, the most likely response from the community of writers will be resentment. As one put it to me:

> No one minds real writing talent being acknowledged, but I find the complete randomness of fame as a writer and associated talent very depressing. Most writers are intensely jealous people.

- For the vast majority of writers, their work is under-rewarded and lonely. As one commented:

> When my first book came out, none of my family seemed quite sure how to react. My husband showed a copy to his parents. They could not have been less interested. My aunt (and godmother) has never mentioned it, although I know my mother has told her about it. None of them have read it. I think they were all rather worried about making me big headed.
>
> The experience taught me a lesson; that what had been my whole life's ambition was in fact a very personal goal, and one that I could not expect anyone else to feel proud of, just for my sake.

The highs of being a writer are undeniable – seeing your book for the first time, a satisfying review, a positive letter from a reader – but they are so utterly unrelated to the really relevant slog of just keeping going.

## Keeping your motivation up and your profile high

These two ambitions seem strongly linked. The very celebrated may bemoan the lack of privacy brought by success, but for the vast majority of writers a little recognition works wonders. Not only is this useful, it's also very motivating.

### Maintaining a public profile

When running publicity campaigns, professionals will try to orchestrate an ongoing sequence of appearances, to build and maintain a profile, rather than a one-off hit at publication time. If you do not have the services of a publicity professional at your disposal to achieve this for you, how can you maintain your profile in between books?

* Aim for a variety of different appearances; don't do too many things at one time. Be selective.
* Be consistent. A letter in a newspaper can be a very effective way of reminding people you are there, but the opposite effect is achieved if your name is always appearing.
* Give talks on your subject matter. Giving a talk on a book you have written exposes you to your market, to those who find the subject (or perhaps just the fact that you have written a book) fascinating. It's also a wonderful way of exploring your own argument, for trying to explain a subject clearly to others is surely the best test of logic. Answering questions at the end of a talk also forces you to reassess trends and examine what is going on right now; to have your own opinions challenged by those with an outlook you do not usually meet in your own social or professional circles. I confess that on such occasions I love the buzz; the reassertion of myself as a writer.

  Talks can be given to schools, to libraries, to literary festivals. Take along leaflets on your books and copies may be bought for the library or you may prompt reader requests. (If you regularly give talks in libraries, think about producing a leaflet listing all the titles you have in print, asking the various publishers involved to make a contribution.)
* Write an article for the *Bookseller* – widely read by book-

sellers who stock your titles as well as other publishers. Or write a piece for the *Author* magazine, *Writers News*, *The Writer* or other magazines read by writers and publishers. (See Useful Addresses.)

- Offer to review books in a publication you would like to be reviewed in yourself. If you have reviewed before, send in samples. If not, write a sample and send it in to illustrate your style. Find out the name of the reviews editor and send it in personally addressed. Remember that controversial opinions are more likely to get noticed, but that memories can be very long – you could be blocking your own future reviewability.

- Write for a newsletter or house magazine – many organisations (public and private) produce them. Can you write a feature to be included (it may have to be for nothing but always ensure you get your 'byline'[1] or name at the end of the piece)? Yearbooks often need relevant articles – can you be included here? In which ones? Start by thinking about those you use yourself on a regular basis, or looking in your local library.

- Write articles for the press – local and national. Again, payment is not certain but the byline is crucial.

- Send information into a gossip column. Most professional magazines have 'people' sections, often passing on trade gossip or announcing promotions. For example, the *Bookseller* has 'Bent's Notes' which appears at the back of the magazine. Most of the photographs sent into such sections are very dull – lots of people lined up with a drink in their hand. So send a photograph (with a caption) with information on you or your book for inclusion (for production reasons the caption needs to be both on the back of the photograph and in the accompanying story).

- Become an after dinner (or after lunch) speaker. Lots of organisations need speakers – and it provides a very useful opportunity to sell copies of your book afterwards. Even better, can you get your book included in the admission price?

[1] Include your name, the name of your book, and the publisher.

- Get your book adopted on a training course and perhaps included in the course price. Delegates love to go away with an 'added value' extra, and your publishers would probably sell at a hefty discount to any organisation taking a bulk order of at least 20 copies.
- Send your CV to programmes on which you would like to be considered as a panellist, for example *Any Questions* or *Front Row* (Radio 4 arts programme).
- Give guest lectures at local colleges and universities. There are now 13 colleges running undergraduate and post-graduate courses in publishing (see Useful Addresses) and many would welcome a talk from a writer on how it feels to be published.
- Give time to a good cause or campaign that has a high public profile. Get involved with one you really believe in and give it full support rather than dabbling in lots of different ones.
- As you become better known you too will be asked for endorsements. Be careful: apply your recommendation without sufficient thought and you risk devaluing your approval; endorse too many things and you can build up media resistance. Don't become a 'rent a quote'.
- Try to stimulate your brain with new ideas. Watch programmes you don't usually see, read a different daily newspaper from your habitual one, go to places you don't usually visit and listen to what other people are saying. Try morning television and see who calls in, or go to a football match and listen. Learn from this. Such events widen your vocabulary and experience of life, and at the same time you may come across new markets for your books, new ways of selling them, as well as new ideas for books.
- Go to exhibitions and galleries. I find wonderful thinking space here, which refreshes my imagination and gives me new ideas – sometimes from watching other people there, looking at the discount structures for admission or just the items for sale in the gift shop.
- Volunteer your services for a judging panel. There are lots of literary competitions today and all need judges who may or may not be remunerated. This keeps your name in the

media, and can be a useful platform for freelance journalism, which again can improve book sales.

## Reminders on this fame business

Being a full-time writer is a life of immense ups and downs. But whilst society loves to knock someone off their plinth, and all the better if you are seen to take yourself too seriously, a writer needs their ego. You need to carry on believing that what you have inside you is worth passing on to other people, and determination to sustain you whilst writing and searching for a publisher. Society expects those who become famous also to be nice, and this can be difficult to keep up in public all the time, particularly if what motivated you to write a book was an old bitterness which the amateur psychiatrist, of which there are so many these days, reckons any sane person would have ditched long ago.

Some writers cope with this by developing a 'writing persona'. On the basis that people take you at your own estimation, they present a character that is interesting to the media and which can be sustained. They are outrageous, melancholic or flirtatious on demand; whatever their 'personality' is reckoned to require. This will be hard work, and may cause internal struggle as the image of the crying clown testifies, but at least as a performance art it can be relinquished on your return home.

The most dangerous thing is to start believing your own publicity. Just because the media is willing to record what you have to say, doesn't mean that you will always say what you mean, or even that they will broadcast what you say. With this in mind, I hope the following piece from journalist and author Celia Brayfield, first published in *The Times*, will be helpful.

# SPOILT BY STARDOM

*Fame should not be a licence to behave boorishly.*

*Fame may be short but life will probably be long, and the successful celebrity knows that it ain't how you start, but how you finish that really counts. For the guidance of the newly famous, therefore, Miss Manners suggests the following:*

*(1) Be nice, especially to your peers. The media will love it if you slag off your fellow artists, but the media don't run the business you are in.*

*(2) Try not to act like a prat. Don't claim special privileges or advertise your limitations.*

*(3) Keep in mind that you are not the only person on the planet.*

*(4) Never, ever write an autobiography. Write a diary instead. Don't admit this until publishers beat down your door, then sit back and collect the royalties in your old age.*

*(5) Have the right friends. The friends who offer to buy your drugs or stage your photo-opportunities will be the ones who shop you to the tabloids and pose for the paparazzi at your funeral.*

*(6) Give back. Never forget that the public think you owe them. Their perception is that you are enjoying unattainable benefits that you don't deserve. Follow the example of Sting or J.K. Rowling: pick at least one charity and support it as visibly and as substantially as you can.*

*(7) If possible, be witty.*

*(8) Learn to say no. You will get more demands on your time, more begging letters and more long-lost rellies coming out of the woodwork than you could possibly imagine. Turn people down gracefully, or create a tsunami of resentment.*

*(9) Remember, you didn't do it all yourself. You did of course. Nobody else wrote that book, played that part or scored that goal. But you've been inappropriately rewarded for it and you must make amends. So when you make your acceptance speech, thank everyone and keep them happy.*

(10) *Sweat the small stuff. One of the myths of being famous is that you will have 'people' who'll take care of everything for you. Many of them take care of themselves first. Check your tax returns, read your balance sheets, get second opinions.*

(11) *Learn the difference between attention and approval (see 1 above). Only do things that gain you approval. Brattish behaviour will only get you attention. Getting attention is not a worthwhile career unless you are two years old or under.*

# Glossary

Much of this appendix originally appeared in *How to Market Books* (Kogan Page, 1999).

**above and below the line** The traditional distinction between different sorts of advertising. 'Above the line' is paid for (for example, space advertisements taken in newspapers). 'Below the line' marketing involves no invoice; it is normally negotiated in a mutually beneficial arrangement between two or more organisations. The usual result is an augmented offer to the consumer (more than just the product being sold), often with a time limit. For example, the offer could invite purchasers of a particular cereal packet to collect coupons by a certain date to secure a further product at a discounted price. Today the distinction between 'above' and 'below' the line is blurring as techniques are used in combination; some marketing agencies now offer 'through the line' services.

**advance notice** (or advance information sheet/forthcoming title sheet) A single sheet giving brief advance details of a forthcoming product. Usually circulated 6–9 months before the item is likely to be available, it is sent to anyone who needs the information – wholesalers, retail outlets, reps, and so on.

**advertorial** Advertising copy that masquerades as an editorial item.

**artwork** Typesetting and illustrations were conventionally pasted onto board to form artwork which could then be photographed to make printing plates. Today most artwork is produced on computer and provided on disk.

**b/w** Abbreviation for black and white.

**bleed** Printed matter that extends over the trimmed edge of the paper; it 'bleeds' off the edge.

**blurb** A short sales message for use in leaflets or on product packaging.

**body copy** The bulk of the advertising text; usually follows the headline.

**brand** A product (or service) with a set of distinct characteristics that make it different from other products on the market.

**bromide** A type of photographic paper.

**bullet point** A heavy dot or other eye-catching feature to attract attention to a shorts sales point. A series of bullet points are often used in advertisement copy:

- good for varying pace and attracting attention
- uneven sentences and surrounding spaces draw in the reader
- allows you to restate the main selling points without appearing overrepetitious.

**camera ready copy** Frequently abbreviated to CRC. Artwork that is ready for photography, reproduction and printing without further alteration.

**centred type** A line or lines of type individually centred on the width of the text below. Type can also be centred on the page width if on a blank page.

**character** An individual letter, space, symbol or punctuation mark.

**coated paper** Paper that has received a coating on one or both sides, for example art paper.

**colour separations** The process of separating the colours of a full-colour picture into four printing colours, done either with a camera or electronic scanning machine. The separated film may then be used to make printing plates.

**competitive differentials** What an organization/ product is good or bad at; the things that set it apart from its competitors.

**copy** Words that make up the message, often used to refer to material prepared for advertising or newspaper features.

**cut-out** An irregularly shaped illustration; will require hand-work at the repro stage of printing.

**design brief** Instructions (preferably written) given to the designer before they start work. The brief should include a description of the market, the objective of the campaign and the budget available.

**desk-top publishing** Producing camera ready copy and artwork on computer screen.

**die-cutting** A specialised cutting process used whenever the requirement for a cut is other than a straight line or right angle (i.e. when a guillotine cannot be used). A metal knife held in wood is punched down onto the item to be cut.

**direct marketing** The selling of services directly to the consumer – can include direct mail, telemarketing, house to house calling, and so on.

**direct response advertising** Advertising designed to produce a measurable response, whether through the mail, telemarketing, space advertisements, or other means. This compares with **direct promotion**, whereby material is sent directly to the market which may, or may not, produce a direct response.

**display type** Large type for headlines, usually 14 point or more.

**dump bin** Container to hold and display stock in retail outlets; usually supplied by the manufacturer to encourage the retailer to take more stock than might otherwise be the case. Most are made from cardboard, to be assembled in the shop.

**duotone** A half-tone shot printed in 2 colours. This is a more expensive way of printing a photograph than simply using a single printing colour, but can add depth and quality to the image presented. It is usually black plus a chosen second colour. An alternative effect can be produced by using a tint of the second colour behind a black and white half-tone.

**embargo** A date before which information may not be released; often used on press releases to ensure that no one paper scoops the rest. Sometimes ignored by the media to secure just such a competitive advantage.

**extent** Length of printed material. For example, for a book, extent: 192pp (192 pages); for a leaflet, extent: 4pp A4 (four sides of A4 paper).

**flush left** (or **justified left**) Type set so that the left-hand margin is vertically aligned, the right-hand margin finishing raggedly wherever the last word ends.

**flush right** (or **justified right**) Type set so that the right-hand margin only is aligned vertically.

**flyer** A cheaply produced leaflet, normally a single sheet for use as a handout.

**font** The range of characters for one size and style of type.

**format** Finished size.

**gsm** (or **g/m²**) The measure by which paper is sold: grams per square metre.

**half-tone** An illustration that reproduces the continuous tone of a photograph. This is achieved by screening the image to break it up into dots. Light areas of the resulting illustration have smaller dots and more surrounding white space to simulate the effect of the original. A **squared-up half-tone** is an image in the form of a box (any shape), as opposed to a **cut-out image**.

**hard copy** Copy on printed paper as opposed to copy on disk or other retrieval system (which is **soft copy**).

**headline** The eye-catching message at the top of an advertisement or leaflet, usually followed by the **body copy**.

**house ad** An advertisement which appears in one of the advertiser's own publications or promotions.

**house style** The typographic and linguistic standards of a particular organisation. For example, there may be a standard way of laying out advertisements, standard typefaces that are always used, and standard rules for spelling and the use of capital letters.

**hype** Short for hyperbole, it literally means exaggerated copy not to be taken seriously. Today it has come to mean over-praising, and is part of the generation of interest in products that appeals to the mass media.

**indent** (1) To leave space at the beginning of a line or paragraph; often used for subheadings and quotations. (2) To order on account; to 'indent for'.

**in-house and out-house work** Jobs that are carried out using either the staff and resources within the firm or those of external companies or freelances.

**insert** Paper or card inserted loose in a book or brochure; not secured in any way.

**ISDN** International standard data number: use of a telephone line for the exchange of data between computers.

**justified type** Type set so that both left- and right-hand margins are aligned vertically – as in newspaper columns.

**lamination** A thin film available in matt or gloss applied to a printed surface; often used for glossy brochures or the covers of catalogues which can expect a lot of wear and tear. Varnishing has a similar effect and is becoming less expensive; it adds less to the bulk than lamination.

**landscape** A format resembling a horizontal oblong, i.e. wider than it is deep (as opposed to **portrait**).

**letterpress** A printing process whereby ink is transferred from raised metal type or plates directly onto paper. All newspapers used to be printed in this way.

**line work** Illustrations such as drawings that consist of lines only, rather than the graduated tones of photographs. The cheapest kind of illustration to reproduce.

**litho** Short for lithographic. A printing process which works on the principle of greasy ink sticking only to those parts of the wet plate which are to be printed. Usually, ink is transferred (offset) from a printing plate onto an intermediary surface ('blanket') and then onto the paper.

**logo** Short for logotype. An identifying symbol or trademark.

**mailshot** A direct marketing message sent through the post.

**measure** The width of text setting, usually measured in pica 'ems' (the 'm' is chosen because it is the widest letter for setting).

**media schedule** Where and when you are planning to advertise.

**merchandising** In a publishing context this means producing branded goods related to a key title and persuading a retailer to stock them, for example a stationery range or soft toy that relates to a popular children's title.

**over-run** (1) Type matter which does not fit the design and must either be cut or the letter and word spacing reduced in size until it fits. (2) Extra copies printed, over and above the quantity ordered from the printer (see **overs**).

**overs** Short for over-run. The practice of printing a slightly larger quantity than ordered to make up for copies spoilt either during printing or binding. It is commercially acceptable for the printer to allow 5 per cent or under the quantity ordered unless otherwise specified. You will be charged for the overs.

**ozalid** A final check before printing, unless a printed proof is requested. An ozalid is a contact paper proof made from the film and usually used as a last-minute check on positioning on complex jobs.

**point of sale** Eye-catching promotional material to be displayed with the product where purchases are made. Examples include showcards, posters, balloons, single copy holders, dump bins and counter packs for display by the till.

**point system** A typographic standard measure based on the pica, for example 12 pt.

**portrait** A format that resembles an upright oblong, i.e. taller than it is wide (see **landscape**).

**pos** Abbreviation for either 'positive' (for example, pos film) or 'point of sale'.

**print run** Number of copies ordered from a printer (see **overs**).

**production specification** The standard to which a product is produced, for example weight of paper to be used, type of envelope in which leaflet is to be inserted.

**progressive proofs** A set of printed proofs showing each colour individually and then in combination.

**proof reading** Reading typeset copy for errors. There are a standard series of proof readers' marks which should be made both by the mistake and in the margin. Typesetters' mistakes should be noted in red, and authors' and publishers' in blue.

**publication date** Publishing term for the date before which books may not be sold, to ensure no one seller saturates the market before all have the same opportunity. Sometimes ignored to secure a competitive advantage.

**recto** The right-hand side of a double page spread (with an odd page number). The opposite of **verso**.

**register** Trim marks should appear on the artwork supplied to a printer, should reappear on the plates made, and need to be matched up when printing to ensure the whole job will be in focus or register. If the plates have not been aligned according to the register marks, or the marks placed incorrectly, the job is said to be 'out of register'.

**repro** Short for reproduction; the conversion of typeset copy and photographs into final film and printing plates.

**response device** How the order or response comes back to the mailer, for example reply card or envelope.

**retouching** Adapting artwork or film to make corrections or alter tonal values.

**reverse out** To produce text as white or a pale colour 'reversed out' of a darker background colour, as opposed to the more usual practice of printing in dark ink on a pale background. This technique can be very effective in small doses, but for lengthy passages of text can be very hard to read.

**roman** Upright type (not bold), as opposed to *italic*.

**run of paper** Refers to the position of an advertisement that will appear in a particular journal or paper wherever there is room, at the editor's or designer's discretion. This is usually cheaper than specifying a particular (or preferred) position.

**saddle stitching** A method of binding pamphlets or small books (64 pages is probably the limit for saddle stitching successfully). Wire staples or thread are used to stitch along the line of the fold. Also called **wire stitching**. For larger publications, the pages are usually trimmed 'flush' and then stuck to a binding (**perfect binding**).

**screen** (1) The process used to convert continuous tone photographs into patterns of dots, in order to reproduce the effect of the original when printed (see **half-tone**). A coarse screen is used in the preparation of illustrations for newsprint and other less demanding jobs. (2) Short for silk screen printing.

**self-mailer** A direct mail piece without an envelope or outer wrapping. Often used to refer to all-in-one leaflets, which combine sales message and response device. Space for copy is limited and so this format works best when the recipient already knows of the product being advertised.

**serif; sans serif** A 'serif' typeface has 'handles' on the letters, like the typeface used in this book; sans serif is the opposite.

**showthrough** Ink on one side of a printed sheet of paper that can be seen through on the other side.

**specs** (1) Short for type specifications. Designers may refer to 'doing the spec', by which they mean laying down the parameters of text design – choosing a typeface and size. (2) The specifications for printing a job are all the production details (format, extent, illustrations, print run, and so on) sent to printers for a quote.

**tag line** (or **strap line**). A line of copy that sums up the product or the general philosophy of the company. Often displayed on the front of the product or packaging, for example book jackets.

**tint** A pattern of dots that when printed reproduces as a tone. Using tints is a good way to get value from your printing inks. For example, even if you only have one printing colour, try putting the text in solid, and using a 10 per cent tint of the same colour to fill in and highlight certain boxes around copy. Further variations can be achieved if you are using more printed colours.

**trim** Short for 'trimmed size' of a printed piece of paper, i.e. its final or guillotined size.

**type area** The area of the final page size that will be occupied by type and illustrations, allowing for the blank border that will normally surround text.

**type face** The style of type, for example Garamond, **Helvetica**.

**type script** The **hard copy** (usually typed or a print out) of the copy to be reproduced and printed.

**typo** Short for typographical error; a mistake in the setting introduced by the typesetter.

**unjustified type** Lines of type set so that the right-hand margin does not align vertically and thus appears ragged. This can also be described as 'ranged left' or 'ragged right'.

**upper and lower case** Upper case characters are CAPITALS, as opposed to lower case.

**verso** The left-hand side of a double page spread (even page numbers). The opposite of **recto**.

**visual, mock up** or **rough layout** A layout of planned printed work showing the position of all the key elements: headlines, illustrations, bullet points, body copy, and so on.

**weight of paper** Paper is sold in varying weights defined in 'gsm' or 'g/m$^2$': grams per square metre. Printers can offer you samples of various papers in different weights.

# Useful Addresses

The Society of Authors
84 Drayton Gardens
London SW10 9SB
tel: 020 7373 6642
fax: 020 7373 5768
website:
www.societyofauthors.org
Professional association for
authors. You are eligible to
join once you have a book
accepted for publication by a
commercial publisher.

The Publishers Association
1 Kingsway
London WC2B 6XF
tel: 020 7565 7474
fax: 020 7836 4543
The trade association of UK
publishers.

International Publishers
Association
Avenue de Miremont 3
CH 1206
Geneva
Switzerland
tel: 01041 22 463018
fax: 01041 22 475717

The Booksellers Association of
Great Britain and Ireland
Minster House
272–74 Vauxhall Bridge Road
London SW1V 1BA
tel: 020 7834 5477
fax: 020 7834 8812
The trade association for over
3,300 member bookshops selling new books.

International Booksellers and
European Booksellers
Federation
34a Rue du Grande Hospice
B-100
Belgium
tel: (0032) 2 223 49 40
fax: (0032) 2 223 49 41
website: www.ebf_eu.org

J Whitaker and Sons Ltd
Endeavour House
189 Shaftesbury Avenue
London WC2H 8JT
tel: 020 7420 6000
editorial fax: 020 7420 6103
As well as producing the
*Bookseller*, Whitaker's editorial department produces a com-

plete list of all titles published in the UK. Publishers are supplied with standard forms and these are returned free of charge; booksellers and libraries pay to access the system in a variety of different formats.

British Council: Publishing Promotion Unit
Bridgewater House
58 Whitworth Street
Manchester M1 6BB
tel: 0161 957 7182
fax: 0161 957 7168
One of the many activities of the British Council is to promote British books abroad. Each year the Council takes exhibition space at over 50 events; they display sample copies of books sent to them by publishers. The Council makes the selection of what to take but there is no charge to publishers for this service.

The Library Association
7 Ridgemount Street
London WC1E 7AE
tel: 020 7636 7543
fax: 020 7436 7218
The professional association for librarians; the LA holds professional examinations, meetings and promotes information on librarianship.

Book Marketing Limited
7a Bedford Square
London WC1B 3RA
tel: 020 7580 7282
fax: 020 7580 7236
Provides research and information on and to the book trade and other interested parties.

Independent Publishers' Guild
Sheila Bounford
4 Middle Street
Great Gransden
Sandy
Beds SG19 3AD
tel: 01767 677753
website: www.ipg.uk.com
Organises regular meetings and attends trade fairs with members' books.

The Society of Freelance Editors and Proofreaders
Mermaid House
Mermaid Court
London SE7 1HR
tel: 020 7403 5141
fax: 020 7407 1193
email:
admin@sfep.demon.co.uk
The SFEP promotes high editorial standards and the professional status of its members.

The Society of Young
Publishers (SYP)
c/o J Whitaker and Sons Ltd
(address above)
Organises monthly meetings
for members of the book trade
under 35 years of age.

Women in Publishing
c/o J Whitaker and Sons Ltd
(address above)
Holds regular meetings for
women working in the pub-
lishing industry.

Data Protection Registrar
Wycliffe House
Water Lane
Wilmslow
Cheshire SK9 5AX
tel: 01625 545745
fax: 01625 524510
For advice on what infor-
mation you can hold on a
database, on whom, and how.

## Training courses for pub-lishers – opportunities for guest speaking

London College of Printing
and Distributive Trades
tel: 020 7514 6700
fax: 020 7514 6772
Runs various courses on printing and production.

London School of Publishing
tel: 020 7221 3399
fax: 020 7243 1730
Runs various courses on printing and production.

Loughborough University,
Department of Information
and Library Studies
tel: 01509 223052
fax: 01509 223053
Publishing available as part of
a degree in library studies.

Middlesex University
tel: 020 8368 1299
fax: 020 8365 1772
Degree course in writing and
publishing; post-graduate
degree course in computer-
integrated publishing.

Napier University
Edinburgh
tel: 0131 444 2266
fax: 0131 452 8532
The Print, Media, Publishing
and Communications Department runs a 3-year BA course
in publishing.

Nottingham Trent University
tel: 0115 948 9467
fax: 0115 948 4266
4-year sandwich course in
Graphic Communications
Management; MAs in
Publishing.

Useful Addresses

Oxford Brookes University
Oxford Centre for Publishing
Studies
tel: 01865 484951
fax: 01865 484952
A 3-year first degree course in
which publishing is studied
along with any other subject
in the modular system; a 9-
month post-graduate diploma
in publishing; and an MA in
electronic media. Also possible
to study publishing skills
through short courses and
evening classes.

The Robert Gordon Institute
of Technology, Aberdeen
tel: 01224 262000
fax: 01224 262969
3-year degree course and 4-year
honours course in publishing
studies.

Thames Valley University,
Ealing
tel: 020 8579 5000
fax: 020 8566 1353
Degree course in information
management and publishing.

University of Leeds
tel: 0113 233 4738
fax: 0113 233 4774
Post-graduate degree course in
bibliography, publishing and
textual studies.

University of Luton
tel: 01582 734111
fax: 01582 489323
3-year course in Media
Practices with Publishing.

University of Plymouth
tel: 01392 475022
fax: 01392 475012
The Faculty of Arts and
Education in Exeter runs a
post-graduate degree, as well
as a post-graduate diploma in
publishing and book
production.

University of Stirling
tel: 01786 467495
fax: 01786 466210
Post-graduate degree or diploma in publishing studies.

West Herts College/University
of Hertfordshire
tel: 01923 257661
fax: 01923 257667
A variety of degree and post-
graduate courses in the
Faculty of Visual
Communication.

## Trade magazines

The Author
The official magazine for the
Society of Authors. See p.141
for details

Books for Keeps
6 Brightfield Road
Lee
London SE12 8QF
tel: 020 8852 4953
fax: 020 8318 7580

Carousel, The Guide to
Children's Books
7 Carrs Lane
Birmingham B4 7TQ
tel: 0121 643 6411
fax: 0121 643 3152

Books Magazine
39 Store Street
London WC1E 3DB
tel: 020 7692 2900
fax: 020 7491 2111

The Bookseller
see J. Whitaker and Sons Ltd,
p. 141.

Publishing News
see *Books Magazine*, above

The School Librarian
The School Library
Association
Liden Library
Barrington Close
Liden
Swindon SN3 6HP
tel: 01793 617838
fax: 01793 537374
Signal (in-depth look at chil-
dren's books in a literary,

educational and historical
context)

Thimble Press
Station Road
South Woodchester
Stroud
Gloucestershire GS5 5EQ
tel: 01453 873 716
fax: 01453 878 599

Writers' Forum
Writers' International Ltd
P.O. Box 3229
Bournemouth
Dorset BH1 1ZS

Writers' News (monthly) and
Writing Magazine (bi-monthly)
Yorkshire Post Newspapers
PO Box 168
Wellington Street
Leeds LS1 1RF
Tel: 0113 238 8333

## Press agencies

Romeike and Curtice
Hale House
Palmers Green
290–296 Green Lanes
London N13 5TP
tel: 020 8882 0155
fax: 020 8882 6716
A useful cuttings service for
spotting reviews and features.

PIMS (UK) Ltd
PIMS House
Mildmay Avenue
London N1 4RS
tel: 020 7226 1000
fax: 020 7704 1360
Can provide a huge variety of
named media contacts, available in a variety of formats,
for example labels or as a
database.

The Press Association
292 Vauxhall Bridge Road
London SW1V 1AE
tel: 020 7963 7000
fax: 020 7963 7594
An extensive domestic news
agency. Send a copy of a press
release on a big story to the
newsdesk and it may end up
being circulated to regional
papers all over the country.
There is no fee but no guaran-
tee the material sent will be
used (same applies to Reuters).

Reuters
85 Fleet Street
London EC4P 4AJ
tel: 020 7250 1122
fax: 020 7542 7921
Reuters are an international
news agency; the London
office receives overseas stories
for distribution in this country.

PR Newswide Europe
210 Old Street
London EC1V 9BR
tel: 020 7490 8111
fax: 020 7490 1255
This is the commercial arm of
the Press Association (formerly
Universal News Services). Send
them a copy of your press
release and they will (for a fee)
circulate it to newsrooms in
Britain (you specify where)
and overseas (due to affilia-
tions with other news associations). The client retains control of how the story is presented in the release.

## Publicists

Colman Getty PR
17-18 Margaret Street
London W1W 8RP
tel: 020 7631 2666
fax: 020 7631 2655

Midas PR
7-8 Kendrick Mews
London SW7 3HG
tel: 020 7584 7474
fax: 020 7584 7123

## Editorial Services

Amolibros
5 Saxon Close
Watchet
Somerset TA23 0BN
tel: 01984 633 713
fax: 01984 633 713

## Obtaining out-of-date newspapers

Historic Newspapers
PO Box 3
Newton Stewart
Wigtownshire DG8 6TQ
tel: 0800 906609
fax: 01988 402 489

# Index

# Acknowledgements

Cover of *Army Wives* by Catherine Jones. Published by Piatkus. Cover photography by Colin Thomas; Art direction by Gary Day-Ellison.

Cover of *Angus, Thongs and Full Frontal Snogging*. Text © Louise Rennison. First published in 1999 by Piccadilly Press Ltd, London. ISBN: 1 8534 05140.

Image taken from the *JoJoMaman Bebe* catalogue. Maternity, baby wear and nursery products by mail order and e-commerce. To request a catalogue call 020 7924 4575 or log on to www.JoJoMamanBebe.co.uk.

*Music Publishing and Patronage - C.F. Peters: 1800 to the Holocaust*. Available from the publisher: Edition Press, 22 Bouverie Gardens, Kenton, Middlesex HA3 ORQ, published February 2000, £25 post free.

*Making it Big in Software* by Peter McHugh. Published in 1999 by Rubic Publishing. Available from www.rubic.co.uk.

*Falling Leaves* press release circulated by Midas Public Relations. www.midaspr.co.uk.

*Girl's Night In* press release circulated by Colman Getty PR. www.colmangettypr.co.uk.

*Mum's New Baby's a Book*. Article published in Camberley News and Mail, 14 December 1990.

Education Direct promotional leaflet. For more information about Education Direct, log on to www.education.co.uk.

Silver Moon Women's Bookshop promotional leaflet. For more information log on to www.silvermoonbookshop.co.uk.

Celia Brayfield's article taken from *The Times*, 24 November 2000. © Celia Brayfield. Information on Celia Brayfield's novels and other writing can be found on her website: www.brayfield.com.

Every effort has been made to trace and acknowledge copyright owners. If any right has been omitted the publishers offer their apologies and will rectify this in subsequent editions following notification.